# DIVINE BREATH

## Unlocking the Ancient Biblical Secret to Transformative Christian Meditation

# DIVINE BREATH

## Unlocking the Ancient Biblical Secret to Transformative Christian Meditation

### Waldemar Zambrano

Revelation Kingdom Inc.

www.revelationkingdom.com

info@revelationkingdom.com

First Edition: 2025

ISBN: HC 979-8-9992088-0-4

ISBN: PB 979-8-9992088-1-1

ISBN: EB 979-8-9992088-2-8

Printed in the United States of America

**Library of Congress Cataloging-in-Publication Data**

## SCRIPTURE PERMISSIONS

This book dedicates itself to all believers seeking a deeper, more intimate relationship with Jesus Christ through the transformative power of biblical meditation and the divine breath that connects us to our Creator.

## CONTACT INFORMATION

For more information about the author, Christian meditation training, or to share your experience with the practices in this book, please visit:

**Christian Meditation Academy**

[www.christianmeditationacademy.com]

[info@christianmeditationacademy.com]

# PREFACE

**"Let the words of my mouth and the meditation of my heart be acceptable in your sight, O LORD, my rock and my redeemer." — Psalm 19:14 (NKJV)**

As I pen these words, I stand in awe of God's intricate tapestry of providence—how He weaves our deepest struggles, darkest moments, and greatest triumphs into a masterpiece that ultimately glorifies Him. Forty years after my first encounter with meditation, I have finally arrived at this sacred moment of fulfillment—the publication of this book that God planted in my heart over two decades ago.

Looking back, I now see how God divinely orchestrated every step of my journey—even those that seemed to lead away from Him—to bring me to this moment. The Lord's words in Jeremiah echo my spirit: **"For I know the plans I have for you… plans to give you hope and a future."** God prepared me to share this message with you after my encounters through church ministry, world travels, military war zones, Christian television ministry, spiritual warfare, and moments of divine revelation.

My spiritual path began as a young man with Hollywood dreams at Columbia College Film School in Chicago back in 1984. Fresh from three years of active Army service as a combat engineer, I carried an unspoken spiritual hunger that would eventually lead me down unexpected paths. Little did I know God would transform my military discipline, honed through twenty-three years of service in the Active Army and National Guard, into a spiritual discipline that would sustain me through the darkest valleys.

At Columbia College, I experienced my first pivotal spiritual awakening. While researching a paper at the Chicago Public Library, my curiosity during a momentary break drew me to the religion section, where I discovered a vast array of books on Eastern religious philosophy and meditation. As a nominal Catholic, I carried a spiritual emptiness I desperately needed to fill. As I read through these Eastern books, the concepts of consciousness, enlightenment, and meditation captivated me, particularly Zen meditation with its disciplined, mindful practice.

With characteristic military discipline, I set myself up for a meditation challenge that would change the trajectory of my life: meditation for six months, every day, for at least four hours, despite working full-time and attending college full-time. I honored this commitment without exception. Meditation became woven into the fabric of my daily life—upon waking, during commutes, and during lunch breaks. Every available moment became an opportunity to sit, close my eyes, and focus on my breath while observing my thoughts. Occasionally, I would open my Bible that I had stored in the dark corner of my closet, reading verses I hoped would keep me grounded in my mediocre faith. Truthfully, I had no clue what was in this incredible book that lay in my hands.

Yet, as the months passed, something remarkable unfolded. As I sat within the stillness of my mind for hours upon hours, the cravings for worldly pleasures that had dominated my life faded like morning mist under the rising sun. The desire to party, steal, lie, cheat, and indulge in pornography—all of it evaporated. I felt a profound purification of my mind, body, and soul. Clarity replaced confusion. Balance replaced chaos. Peace replaced my inner turmoil. Once hardened by life's disappointments, my stone-cold heart softened with newfound compassion and love. I would later conclude that I had reached the level of truly walking in the spirit. When my six-month challenge ended, the transformation was undeniable.

I'm not sharing this to promote Eastern meditation practices. Instead, I'm revealing to you what happened to me through a structured, committed mindfulness meditation practice, which resulted in a mind-blowing transformation and renewal of my life.

Yet, at this spiritual crossroads, I faced an unexpected decision: continue down this path, which would inevitably convert me into an urban monk, or break off from my intense meditation practice and pursue my desire for marriage and family.

As amazing as the experience was, I sensed something profound within my spirit, whispering that something vital was still missing—what I would later discover to be the Holy Spirit living within me through the resurrection power of Jesus Christ.

I ultimately reduced my meditation practice and gradually returned to my old ways. I married, raised a family, and joyfully accepted Jesus Christ as my Lord and Savior. The Lord's hand guided me away from those Hollywood aspirations and blessed me with twenty years of service in a Christian television ministry based in Chicago. I produced and directed Christian programming that affected people's lives and connected me with remarkable Christian leaders worldwide—all part of God's preparation for the message I now share with you.

Yet even though I served in church and television ministry and attended Moody Bible Institute's certification training, that annoying, sinful nature, which I thought I'd conquered when I became a born-again believer, slowly but surely exerted its influence on me. I attempted to combat my dark, sinful nature with hours of personal time praying, doing Bible studies, listening, and watching all forms of media related to ministries to strengthen my spiritual walk with God. But somehow, these dark tendencies persisted despite my efforts and relationship with the Holy Spirit.

My life suddenly turned unexpectedly in 2003 when my National Guard unit deployed to Iraq. There, in the crucible of war, I encountered dark spiritual forces that nearly destroyed me physically and mentally. In April 2003, our unit arrived in Kuwait, a surreal experience of white desert sands and tent cities housing over 200,000 soldiers. We remained there temporarily until receiving orders to advance into Iraq.

During this waiting period, something inexplicable occurred. While cleaning up after a command briefing one day, I was straightening the central command table when suddenly, without warning, I inhaled some vaporous substance that forced its way down my throat and into my lungs. The sensation was like swallowing tiny bits of shattered glass. I bolted from the tent, heaving and vomiting uncontrollably. "What in God's name was that?" I thought to myself. It took me a bit of time to clear my throat, and instead of learning my lesson the first time, curiosity overcame caution.

I slowly returned to the command tent to investigate. I cautiously circled the tent area and found no visible vapor or particles in the air. That was until I arrived at the exact spot where I had my first encounter: the mysterious particles reared their ugly head and rushed into my lungs again, causing me to rush back outside to heave and choke. This time, as much as I tried to clear my lungs of the particles, it was fruitless.

This began a nightmare of physical and mental suffering. I refused to seek medical attention because I was my unit's assigned acting First Sergeant. My top priority was my commitment to my soldiers; I feared they would take me away to be hospitalized and medicated. Instead, I turned to God as my healer, and I would stick to that to the end.

Each night that presented itself before me brought even greater torment. Lying down triggered violent heaving and choking. Frustrated, I would rise in the middle of the night, step out into the barren desert with my CD player, and play Michael W. Smith's worship music under the vast starlit sky. While my fellow soldiers slept, I stood alone in the desert, arms raised to heaven, worshipping and pleading with God for healing.

For eleven excruciating days, I suffered from this mysterious affliction that felt like tiny glass shards embedded in my lungs. As we convoyed across the border into Iraq and established our position at Al Taji, a former Republican Guard base near Baghdad, my physical condition deteriorated further. Sleepless nights took their toll. My mind and body were breaking down under the combined stress of my mysterious ailment and the realities of being in a combat zone. Now I spent my nights on the rooftop of our dwelling space, looking up into the vast universe, crying to God to heal me!

On the eleventh day of my affliction, everything finally came to the climactic spiritual battle I had not expected. Physically and mentally exhausted, I staggered into my quarters to rest. Suddenly, out of the blue, one of my hands began trembling uncontrollably. Watching a part of your body react without your permission was the strangest sensation. Then, the other hand started shaking uncontrollably. Soon, tormenting voices surrounded me, taunting me that I wouldn't survive, that I would die in Iraq and never see my family again. My entire body began convulsing. Sweating and crying, I collapsed onto my cot, curling into a fetal position, begging God to take my life. I didn't want to live anymore!

In this moment of complete surrender, when I had reached my absolute limit, God revealed the profound connection between breath and spirit that would become the foundation of this book. The maddening, tormenting voices ceased, and came the gentle voice of the Holy Spirit. "Waldemar, just breathe." Just breathe? I thought to myself. That was strange. What have I been doing all this time? I was breathing. The Holy Spirit's voice came upon me again. "Waldemar, just breathe."

I remembered my meditation challenge from college: sit in stillness, breathe slowly and deeply into the belly area, being mindful of my thoughts. So, I acted and lay myself flat on my cot, face up. I stared at the ceiling nervously and inhaled slowly, deeply, through my nostrils. Do you know what happened? Did I go into a pleasant state of peaceful rest? Absolutely not; A surge of jolting electricity shot through my body. It was so powerful that it lifted me from my cot and tossed me on the hard concrete floor. "What in God's name is happening to me?" I thought to myself. Then I realized. I had a damaged nervous system, and the Holy Spirit revealed to me the need for a reset.

So, I crawled back up onto my cot and tried again. Excruciating, jolting pain greeted me, but I persisted and continued to breathe through it. Eventually, the shattered glass-like sensation in my lungs dissolved until I could finally take a slow, deep inhale. Do you know what happened next? Yes, peace washed over me this time, and I fell into a deep, restorative sleep, awakening six hours later completely healed. Praise God!!

This profound experience became the genesis of my journey into Christian meditation and breathwork. I discovered that the breath—this simple, fundamental aspect of human existence—could be a powerful conduit for God's healing presence. The Holy Spirit used my breath as a vehicle for divine intervention, revealing that profound spiritual experiences often come through the most basic physical processes.

In the years that followed, I began studying Scripture with a fresh perspective, discovering the vibrant biblical theology of breath—from God breathing life into Adam in Genesis to Jesus breathing the Holy Spirit upon his disciples in John. What I experienced in Iraq wasn't merely a personal healing technique but a rediscovery of an ancient spiritual truth: our breath connects us to the very breath of God.

My earlier explorations of Eastern meditation had led me into dangerous spiritual territory, where dark forces sought to derail God's purpose for my life. Yet even these detours were part of His sovereign plan. Through them, I learned to discern the critical differences between Eastern practices that empty the mind and biblical meditation that fills it with God's truth. As Psalm 1:1-3 declares:

**"Blessed is the man who walks not in the counsel of the ungodly, nor stands in the path of sinners, nor sits in the seat of the scornful, but his delight is in the LAW of the Lord, and His LAW, he MEDITATES day and night. He shall be like a tree planted by the rivers of water that bring forth its fruit in its season, whose leaf also shall not wither; And whatever he does shall prosper." (NKJV)**

This book represents the culmination of a forty-year journey—from spiritual hunger to divine fulfillment, from Eastern practices to biblical truth, from military battlefields to spiritual warfare. It is a testimony of what God has done in my life and a prophetic invitation to what He desires to do in yours. Through these pages, I share the transformative practice of Christian meditation with the power of the Breath of Life, which God revealed through hardship, healing, and the Holy Spirit's guidance.

You are about to embark on an incredible journey of discovery that will transform your spiritual walk with God. As founder of the Christian Meditation Academy, I now fulfill God's calling to train and unite believers seeking spiritual transformation through authentic Christian meditation practices that deepen our connection with the Holy Spirit and cultivate lives that honor God.

I am truly humbled that God chose me, with all my flaws and detours, to bring this message to you. May the divine breath that first animated humanity continue to flow through each of us, bringing life, healing, and transformation to a world gasping for spiritual oxygen.

# INTRODUCTION:
# The Journey Begins

Welcome to an incredible journey that will transform your spiritual life through the ancient practice of biblical meditation. This book is not just a collection of information—it's a pathway to a deeper, more vibrant relationship with God through the power of biblical meditation and the revelations hidden within Hebrew and Greek words and letters.

As you embark on this journey, you are taking a crucial step in your spiritual walk with the Holy Spirit. Many Christians today struggle with stress, anxiety, addictions, and the persistent pull of their sinful nature. Despite faithful church attendance, Bible reading, and prayer, something seems to be missing—a deeper connection, a more transformative experience of God's presence.

For many believers, the missing element is a proper understanding and practice of meditation. While the world has embraced various forms of meditation for mental health and spiritual exploration, many Christians have shied away from this practice, fearing its association with Eastern religions. Yet the Bible mentions meditation at least twenty-five times and presents it as essential for spiritual growth, prosperity, and success.

## INTRODUCTION:
### The Journey Begins

**"This book of the law must not depart from your mouth; you are to meditate on it day and night so that you may carefully observe everything written in it. For then, you will prosper and succeed in whatever you do." Joshua 1:8 (NKJV)**

At first glance, the command to meditate day and night may seem daunting, perhaps even impossible. How can anyone with a busy life—career, family, social obligations—possibly fulfill such a requirement? The answer lies in understanding biblical meditation beyond the simplified notion of merely repeating Scripture verses.

# The Purpose of This Book

This book will take you on a progressive journey of discovery, revealing the profound truths about Christian meditation through the lens of Hebrew and Greek words and letters. You will learn:

1. What meditation truly means according to God's Word is beyond many Christians' limited understanding today.
2. The Hebrew words Hagah, Siyach, and Higgayon, as well as the Greek word Meletao, reveal a much richer understanding of meditation.
3. The powerful connection between the breath of life, the Holy Spirit, and your meditation practice.
4. Practical, transformative Christian meditation techniques that will strengthen your spiritual walk.
5. How to develop a sustainable meditation practice that fits into your daily life.

6. The mystical meanings of Hebrew letters and how they can deepen your meditation experience.

By the end of this book, you will have a comprehensive understanding of biblical meditation and a practical framework for implementing it in your life. You will discover how to move from a state of meditative unconsciousness—where you drift through life on spiritual autopilot—to a state of meditative consciousness, where you are fully aware of God's presence and guidance moment by moment.

# How to Use This Book

I recommend setting aside dedicated time each day to read and practice the meditation techniques presented to get the most out of this journey. As you read the book from beginning to end, each chapter progressively builds on the previous one, creating a transformative experience.

We divided the book into three main parts.

**Part I: Foundations of Christian Meditation** explores what meditation truly is according to both the world and the Bible, revealing the profound insights hidden in Hebrew and Greek words.

**Part II: The Breath of Life** delves into the connection between breath, spirit, and meditation, introducing you to the concept of meditative consciousness and the role of the Holy Spirit.

**Part III: The Transformational Journey** presents a comprehensive framework for Christian meditation, with specific applications for spiritual warfare, divine revelation, and healing. It also provides guidance for building a sustainable practice and sharing it with others.

Throughout the book, you will find practical meditation exercises, scriptural insights, and personal reflections to help you integrate these teachings into your life. The Hebrew letter graphics and their meanings will provide visual anchors for your meditation practice, connecting you to the ancient wisdom in God's Word.

# A Personal Invitation

As you begin this journey, I invite you to approach it with an open heart and mind. Some concepts may challenge your previous understanding, while others will affirm what you've always known to be true. Throughout it all, I encourage you to test everything against Scripture and to rely on the Holy Spirit's guidance.

Remember that meditation is not about emptying your mind, but filling it with God's truth. It's not about escaping reality, but about engaging more fully with the reality of God's presence in every moment. It's not about achieving some mystical state, but developing a more intimate relationship with the living God.

The journey ahead will require commitment, but the rewards are immeasurable. As you learn to meditate according to biblical principles, you will find yourself more attuned to God's voice, more resistant to temptation, more peaceful during life's storms, and more effective in your spiritual walk.

## INTRODUCTION:
## The Journey Begins

So, take a deep breath—the breath of life that God has given you—and let's begin this transformative journey together. The ancient practice of Christian meditation awaits, ready to reveal its treasures to those willing to explore its depths.

May the Holy Spirit guide, teach, and transform you as you discover the hidden power of Christian meditation through Hebrew and Greek revelations. Let the journey begin.

# CHAPTER ONE:
# The Lost Art of Biblical Meditation

In today's fast-paced world, with its many distractions and short attention spans, most people have forgotten an ancient spiritual practice among Christians. Once, early Christians considered biblical meditation essential to spiritual growth, yet many modern believers misunderstood or avoided it. What has happened to this powerful spiritual discipline, God commanded His people to practice?

## The Modern Misconception

When most Christians today hear the word "meditation," their minds often jump to images of cross-legged practitioners chanting mantras, Eastern religious practices, or New Age spirituality. This association has created a fear among many believers about embracing meditation as a spiritual practice. Some churches have labeled all forms of meditation as dangerous or unbiblical, creating a significant barrier to recovering this lost art.

This misconception represents one of the enemy's most successful strategies: taking a God-ordained practice and associating it so thoroughly with a counterfeit spirituality that God's people fear what it blessed them. The result is that many Christians have unwittingly surrendered a powerful spiritual tool God intended for their prosperity, success, and spiritual growth.

In his book "The Missing Link of Meditation," Pastor Bill Winston boldly states: "Apart from hearing God's Word preached and read, meditation is the most important and powerful ingredient for spiritual growth and success." He further emphasizes, "Meditation is a spiritual law, and it works!" Yet, despite such endorsements from respected Christian leaders, meditation remains underutilized in most believers' spiritual arsenals.

# What the World Thinks Meditation Is

To understand how we've arrived, let's first examine how the world defines meditation. Merriam-Webster's Dictionary defines meditation as:

1. To engage in contemplation or reflection.
2. Engaging in mental exercise (such as concentrating on one's breathing or repeating a mantra) to reach a heightened level of spiritual awareness.
3. To focus one's thoughts on, reflect on, or ponder.
4. To plan or project in mind: Intend or purpose.

The American Psychological Association further expands this definition, describing meditation as "profound and extended contemplation or reflection to achieve focused attention or an otherwise altered state of consciousness and gain insight into oneself and the world." They also note that, while traditionally associated with spiritual and religious exercises, people now use meditation for relaxation, stress relief, and to promote overall health and well-being.

The Oxford Dictionary adds that meditation involves "focusing your mind, usually in silence, especially for religious reasons or to calm your mind."

These secular definitions highlight several key aspects of meditation: contemplation, focus, mental exercise, and pursuing calm or spiritual awareness. While these elements aren't inherently problematic, they present an incomplete picture of biblical meditation, focusing primarily on technique rather than a relationship with God.

# Historical Perspectives on Meditation

An examination of earlier definitions of meditation surprisingly reveals a perspective more aligned with biblical understanding. Webster's Dictionary of 1828 defined meditation as:

1. To dwell on anything in thought; to contemplate; to study; to turn over or revolve any subject in mind; appropriately, but not only used by pious contemplation or consideration of the great truths of religion.
2. To intend; to have contemplation.
3. To plan by revolving in mind, to contrive, to intend.

This earlier definition explicitly connects meditation with "pious contemplation," and "the great truths of religion," even citing **Psalm 1:2** as an example: **"His delight is in the law of the Lord, and His Law, he meditates day and night." (NKJV)**

Broader cultural changes are shifting how we define and perceive meditation. As Western society has become more secular and Eastern spiritual practices have gained popularity, the understanding of meditation has moved away from its biblical roots. This cultural shift has left many Christians uncertain about how to reclaim this practice in a way that honors God.

# Why Christians Have Avoided Meditation

The avoidance of meditation among Christians stems from several factors:

1. **Fear of Eastern Religious Influence:** Many Christians worry that any form of meditation will open them to Eastern religious influences or even demonic activity. This fear is intense regarding practices that involve quieting the mind or controlled breathing, which are common elements in both Eastern meditation and, as we'll discover, biblical meditation as well.

2. **Lack of teaching:** Few churches provide clear, biblical meditation instruction. Without proper instruction, believers don't know how to practice meditation as Scripture teaches.

3.  **Confusion About Method**: The simplified instruction to "take a Bible verse and revolve it in your mind until a spiritual truth arises" leaves many Christians confused about the practical aspects of meditation. Without a clear framework, the practice remains abstract and inaccessible.

4.  **Time Constraints**: The biblical command to meditate "day and night" (Joshua 1:8) can seem overwhelming in our busy world. Many believers dismiss meditation as impractical, given their hectic schedules.

5.  **Misunderstanding of Purpose**: Some Christians view meditation as merely an intellectual exercise rather than a transformative spiritual practice that engages the whole person—spirit, soul, and body.

These barriers have collectively contributed to the loss of biblical meditation as a central spiritual discipline in many believers' lives. Yet, as we'll discover throughout this book, meditation, as described in Scripture, is distinct from Eastern practices and essential for spiritual growth and maturity.

# Voices of Modern Christian Leaders on Meditation

Despite the general avoidance of meditation in many Christian circles, several prominent Christian leaders have recognized its importance and advocated for its recovery:

# CHAPTER ONE:
## The Lost Art of
## Biblical Meditation

Charles Stanley asserts, "I'm convinced that the man who has learned to meditate upon the Lord will be able to run on his feet and walk in his spirit." This powerful statement highlights how meditation enables believers to maintain spiritual vitality despite life's demands.

Watchman Nee offers this profound insight: "Take this as the secret of Christ's life in you: His Spirit dwells in your innermost Spirit. Meditate on it, believe in it, and remember it until this glorious truth produces a holy fear and wonder that the Holy Spirit indeed abides in you." Here, Nee points to meditation to deepen our awareness of the Holy Spirit's indwelling presence.

In his bestselling book *The Purpose Driven Life*, Rick Warren writes, "Focused thinking is meditation. It takes serious effort. You select a verse and reflect on it repeatedly in your mind... if you know how to worry, you already know how to meditate." Warren's practical approach helps demystify meditation for modern believers.

Timothy Keller explains, "Meditation is taking a truth and thinking—applying it to yourself, personally, bearing down on your own heart with it." This definition emphasizes the personal, transformative nature of biblical meditation.

These contemporary voices join with historical Christian figures like Thomas à Kempis, who wrote in "The Imitation of Christ": "It is better to feel contrition than to know its definition... If you knew the whole Bible by heart and the philosophers' sayings, what would this profit you without

God's love and grace? Shut your door upon yourself and call Jesus your Beloved. Stay with Him in your cell, for you will not find such peace elsewhere."

The consistent message from these spiritual leaders is clear: meditation is not an optional add-on to the Christian life, but a central discipline for spiritual formation and growth.

# Reclaiming the Lost Art

As we begin our journey to reclaim the lost art of biblical meditation, we recognize that we're not introducing something new to Christianity, but recovering something ancient and essential. Scripture weaves the Biblical practice of meditation throughout its text, from Joshua's instruction to meditate on the Law Day and night to David's many references to meditation in the Psalms and to Paul's exhortation to Timothy to "meditate on these things."

In the following chapters, we will explore the rich biblical understanding of meditation through the lens of Hebrew and Greek words. We'll discover that meditation is far more than just repeating Scripture verses—it encompasses our entire moment-by-moment consciousness. It provides a pathway to deeper communion with God through the Holy Spirit.

The journey to reclaim biblical meditation begins with openness — a willingness to set aside preconceptions and explore what Scripture actually teaches about this vital practice. It requires courage to move beyond cultural barriers and embrace God's ordained discipline for our spiritual prosperity.

# CHAPTER ONE:
## The Lost Art of
## Biblical Meditation

As we proceed, remember that the goal of biblical meditation is not to achieve some mystical state or to gain esoteric knowledge. Instead, it is to deepen our relationship with God, to align our thoughts with His truth, and to live in constant awareness of His presence. It is about learning to abide in Christ moment by moment, day by day.

The lost art of biblical meditation awaits rediscovery. Let us approach this with humility, expectancy, and an intense desire to experience the extraordinary fullness of what God intended when He commanded His people to meditate on His Law Day and night.

# CHAPTER TWO:
# The Secret Revelation:
## Understanding Biblical Meditation

Now, let's embark on our journey of discovery with the first revelation. We will explore a Biblical verse where God unveils a unique perspective on meditation. Prepare to be enlightened as we uncover a profound truth hidden in plain sight for centuries.

**"Blessed is the man who walks not in the counsel of the ungodly, nor stands in the path of sinners, nor sits in the seat of the scornful, but his delight is in the LAW of the Lord, and in His LAW, he MEDITATES DAY AND NIGHT. He shall be like a tree planted by the rivers of water that bring forth its fruit in its season, whose leaf also shall not wither; And whatever he does shall prosper." Psalm 1:1-3 (NKJV)**

"Meditate day and night on the Law?" Really? How on earth am I supposed to do that? I have a life to live… I have a job, a social life, a career, a business, school, and family. How can God expect me to murmur or repeatedly recite a Bible verse all day? It makes no sense if we interpret biblical meditation as it presents itself to us through the current translation.

So, to fix that, we will look at the keyword LAW to answer what God meant when he said to meditate day and night. The Hebrew word used for Law is **Torah (תּוֹרָה)**, which carries a much richer meaning than our English translation suggests. Torah is not merely a set of rigid rules, but encompasses

**teachings, instructions, and guidance**. It's a root word that reveals God's heart toward His people, not to burden them with regulations, but to provide a pathway for abundant living.

Now let's look at the same verse we just read, with the word **LAW** bolded, and next to it, the three additional words that, according to Biblical scholars, fit more appropriately with this verse. These alternative translations help us understand God's communication more fully. Let's look:

**"Blessed is the man who walks not in the counsel of the ungodly, nor stands in the path of sinners, nor sits in the seat of the scornful, but his delight is in the TEACHINGS/INSTRUCTIONS/GUIDANCE of the Lord, And in His TEACHINGS/INSTRUCTIONS/GUIDANCE he MEDITATES Day and night. He shall be like a tree planted by the rivers of water that brings forth its fruit in its season, whose leaf also shall not wither; And whatever he does shall prosper." Psalm 1:1-3 (NKJV)**

See the difference that makes? This is a powerful Bible verse with incredible layers of wisdom and knowledge that we must take to heart. The verse doesn't instruct us to revolve around a Bible verse in our minds until spiritual truth is revealed. Here, we meditate throughout the day. I will explain what this means in a few moments. The Bible verse tells us how, as we walk through our day, not to take the advice of ungodly people who run across our path, nor stand in a pathway with people who try to tempt us to sin, nor hang out with those who badmouth or speak things that could prompt bad intentions on our part. It tells us to be delighted and to MEDITATE, in our case, on the Holy Spirit's teachings, guidance, and instructions all day and night! Got it?

# Understanding Your Moment-to-Moment State

Every human being exists in one of two states at any moment: meditative consciousness or meditative unconsciousness. These terms may sound complex, but they describe a reality we all experience daily.

Meditative consciousness is a state of spiritual awareness and present-moment attention. It's being fully awake to God's presence, aware of your thoughts and emotions, and attentive to the Holy Spirit's teachings, instructions, and guidance. In this state, you're engaged with reality, not as your mind distorts it through fears, assumptions, or habitual patterns.

Meditative unconsciousness is a state of spiritual autopilot. It involves moving through life with minimal awareness, allowing your thoughts, emotions, and actions to be driven by unconscious patterns, cultural programming, and your sinful nature. In this state, you're technically awake but spiritually asleep, unaware of God's presence, and unresponsive to the Holy Spirit's teachings, guidance, and instructions.

The distinction between these states is not merely theoretical—it has profound implications for your spiritual life, relationships, and effectiveness in God's kingdom. As Jesus warned in

**Matthew 24:42, "Therefore stay awake, for you do not know on what day your Lord is coming."** This call to "stay awake" is an exhortation to maintain meditative consciousness rather than drifting into unconsciousness.

# The Biblical Precedent for Continuous Awareness

This concept of continuous spiritual awareness extends beyond Psalm 1. Throughout Scripture, we find this theme repeated:

- **Joshua 1:8** — "This Book of the Law shall not depart from your mouth, but you shall meditate on it day and night, so that you may be careful to do according to all that is written in it."
- **Psalm 119:97** — "Oh, how I love your law! It is my meditation all day."
- **Proverbs 3:6** — "In all your ways acknowledge him, and he will make straight your paths."
- **Colossians 3:2** — "Set your minds on things that are above, not on things that are on earth."
- **Philippians 4:8** — "Finally, brothers, whatever is true, whatever is honorable, whatever is just, whatever is pure, whatever is lovely, whatever is commendable, if there is any excellence, if there is anything worthy of praise, think about these things."

These verses collectively paint a picture of the meditative consciousness God calls us to—a continuous awareness of His presence and truth that informs every aspect of our lives.

# The Danger of Spiritual Autopilot

Most people spend most of their waking hours in a state of meditative unconsciousness—on spiritual autopilot. This state's characteristics include:

1. **Reactive Patterns**: Responding to situations based on ingrained habits rather than conscious choice.
2. **Mental Wandering**: Allowing the mind to drift aimlessly between past regrets and future anxieties.
3. **Emotional Triggering**: Being easily provoked into emotional reactions without awareness or self-regulation.
4. **Spiritual Dullness**: Failing to perceive God's presence or activity in daily life.
5. **Physical Disconnection**: Being unaware of bodily sensations, including the breath that connects you to God.
6. **Relational Blindness**: Interacting with others based on projections rather than truly seeing them as they are.
7. **Environmental Obliviousness**: Moving through creation without noticing its beauty or receiving its testimony about God.

# CHAPTER TWO:
## The Secret Revelation: Understanding Biblical Meditation

This state's danger is impossible to exaggerate. When we operate on spiritual autopilot, we're vulnerable to the enemy's schemes, prone to act from our sinful nature rather than the Spirit, and likely to miss divine appointments and opportunities.

Consider a common experience: driving a familiar route while lost in thought, suddenly realizing you've arrived at your destination with no memory of the journey. Your body performed all the necessary actions—turning the wheel, pressing the pedals, observing traffic signals — while your conscious mind was elsewhere. This physical autopilot is a perfect analogy for the spiritual autopilot that characterizes meditative unconsciousness.

Just as driving on autopilot increases the risk of accidents, living on spiritual autopilot increases the risk of spiritual casualties. The unconscious mind, influenced by the sinful nature and worldly programming, makes choices that the conscious, Spirit-led mind would reject. This explains why believers often think, say, or do things that contradict their conscious values and commitments.

Paul describes this struggle in **Romans 7:15: "I do not understand what I do. For what I want to do, I do not do, but what I hate, I do." (NIV)** This Internal conflict often stems from the disconnect between our conscious intentions (formed in meditative consciousness) and our unconscious actions (flowing from meditative unconsciousness).

# Jesus's Call to "Stay Awake"

Throughout His ministry, Jesus repeatedly emphasized the importance of spiritual wakefulness—what we're calling meditative consciousness. His exhortations to "stay awake" appear in various contexts:

In the Olivet Discourse, Jesus warns about His return: **"Therefore, stay awake, for you do not know on what day your Lord is coming" Matthew 24:42. (ESV)** He continues with the parable of the ten virgins, concluding, **"Watch therefore, for you know neither the day nor the hour" Matthew 25:13. (ESV)**

In Gethsemane, Jesus finds His disciples sleeping and admonishes them: **"Watch and pray that you may not enter into temptation. The spirit indeed is willing, but the flesh is weak" Matthew 26:41 (ESV)**. This statement directly connects spiritual wakefulness with resistance to temptation.

In Mark's Gospel, Jesus broadens this call to all believers: **"And what I say to you, I say to all: Stay awake" Mark 13:37 (ESV)** This universal command shows that meditative consciousness is not just for spiritual elites, but for every follower of Christ.

The Greek word translated as **"stay awake" or "watch"** in these passages is **grēgoreō**, which means to be **awake or vigilant** but metaphorically conveys a sense of spiritual alertness and readiness. This is the opposite of meditative unconsciousness—it's a heightened awareness of spiritual realities and a divine presence.

Jesus's emphasis on staying awake reveals that meditative consciousness is not optional for believers but is essential for spiritual survival and effectiveness. It's the state in which we can discern God's voice, resist temptation, and respond appropriately to divine opportunities.

## Recognizing Spiritual Warfare in Daily Life

One of the primary reasons Jesus calls us to stay awake is the reality of spiritual warfare. The apostle Peter warns, **"Be sober-minded; be watchful. Your adversary, the devil, prowls around like a roaring lion, seeking someone to devour" 1 Peter 5:8 (ESV).** The command to be "watchful" (again, grēgoreō) directly connects spiritual wakefulness with readiness for warfare.

We become easy targets for the enemy's schemes when we drift into meditative unconsciousness. Meditative unconsciousness lowers our defenses, dulls our discernment, and drives our responses by pre-programmed patterns rather than Spirit-led wisdom. It's like a soldier falling asleep at his post—a dangerous vulnerability in a combat zone.

Dramatic confrontations with demonic forces do not limit this state; Paul acknowledges this reality in **2 Corinthians 10:3-5: "For though we walk in the flesh, we are not waging war according to the flesh. The weapons of our warfare are not of the flesh, but have divine power to destroy strongholds. We destroy arguments and every lofty opinion raised against the knowledge of God and take every thought captive to obey Christ." (ESV)**

The battlefield is primarily in the mind, within the realm of thoughts, beliefs, and perceptions. This is precisely why meditative consciousness is so crucial. In this state, we can identify thoughts that contradict God's truth, emotions that signal spiritual attack, and desires that originate from the sinful nature rather than the Spirit.

Consider how different spiritual warfare unfolds depending on your state:

**In meditative unconsciousness**, a critical thought about another believer quickly spirals into judgment, gossip, and division—precisely what the enemy desires.

**In meditative consciousness,** one recognizes the same initial thought as potentially destructive, examines it in light of Scripture, and replaces it with grace and prayer, thwarting the enemy's scheme**.**

**In meditative unconsciousness**, a trigger for anxiety activates a cascade of worry, fear, and worst-case scenarios that paralyze faith and action.

**In meditative consciousness,** one acknowledges the exact trigger, surrenders it to God, and counters it with a biblical truth that maintains peace and enables wise action.

The difference is not in the initial thought or trigger—these may be similar in both states—but in the level of awareness and the quality of response. Meditative consciousness provides the spiritual alertness necessary **to "stand against the devil's schemes" (Ephesians 6:11).**

# The Holy Spirit's Role In Conscious Living

While Jesus commands us to stay awake, He doesn't expect us to maintain meditative consciousness through sheer willpower. The Holy Spirit is crucial in awakening and sustaining our spiritual awareness.

Jesus promises that the Holy Spirit will **"teach you all things and bring to your remembrance all that I have said to you"** (John 14:26) and **"guide you into all the truth"** (John 16:13). These functions of teaching, reminding, and guiding are essential for maintaining meditative consciousness.

The Holy Spirit is our internal alarm system, alerting us when we drift unconscious. Paul refers to this in **Romans 8:16: "The Spirit himself bears witness with our spirit that we are children of God." (ESV)** The Spirit's witness isn't just a one-time assurance of salvation but an ongoing communion that keeps us spiritually alert and aware of our identity in Christ.

Paul also describes the Spirit's role in conscious living in **Galatians 5:16-18: "But I say, walk by the Spirit, and you will not gratify the desires of the flesh. For the desires of the flesh are against the Spirit, and the desires of the Spirit are against the flesh, for these are opposed to each other, to keep you from doing the things you want to do. But if the Spirit leads you, you are not under the law." (ESV)**

"**Walking by the Spirit**" is essentially living in meditative consciousness—being aware of and responsive to the Spirit's presence and guidance moment by moment. This state doesn't eliminate the desires of the flesh (they remain "opposed to each other"), but it enables us to recognize those desires for what they are and choose to follow the Spirit instead.

The Holy Spirit also empowers our conscious living through the fruit He produces: **"love, joy, peace, patience, kindness, goodness, faithfulness, gentleness, self-control" (Galatians 5:22-23).** Human effort did not generate these qualities, but they emerge naturally when we remain in meditative consciousness, aware of and yielding to the Spirit's work.

## Practical Steps to Cultivate Meditative Consciousness

How can we move from the default state of meditative unconsciousness to the spiritually vibrant state of meditative consciousness? Here are practical steps to cultivate greater awareness:

1. **Begin with Breath Awareness: As explored in the previous chapter, the spirit intimately connects with breath.** Begin each day with a few minutes of conscious breathing, remembering that each breath is God's gift and a reminder of the Spirit's presence within you.

2. **Practice Present-Moment Attention**: Intentionally bring your attention to the present moment throughout the day. Notice the sensations in your body, the surrounding sounds, and the thoughts passing through your mind. This practice of presence counters the mind's tendency to dwell in the past or future.

3. **Implement Pattern Interrupts**: create triggers that remind you to return to consciousness. For example, when your phone rings, take a deep breath and silently say, "Holy Spirit, I'm listening." These pattern interrupts help break the spell of unconsciousness.

4. **Develop Thought Awareness**: Practice observing your thoughts without immediately identifying them. When a thought arises, ask: "Is this from the Spirit or another source? Does this align with God's truth?" This discernment is essential for taking thoughts captive.

5. **Engage in Scripture Meditation**: Regularly meditate on God's Word using our explored Hebrew and Greek approaches. This practice anchors your consciousness in

divine truth and trains your mind to recognize deviations from that truth.

6. **Cultivate Emotional Intelligence**: Learn to recognize emotions as they arise, naming them specifically and exploring their sources. Emotional awareness prevents unconscious reactions and creates space for Spirit-led responses.

7. **Practice Body Awareness**: Throughout the day, notice sensations in your body, especially tension or discomfort. The body often signals spiritual and emotional states before the conscious mind recognizes them.

8. **Establish Accountability**: Share your journey toward meditative consciousness with close, trusted spiritual companions who can help you recognize your unconsciousness.

9. **Create Environmental Reminders**: Place visual cues in your home, workplace, and digital spaces that prompt you to return to awareness. These might be Scripture verses, meaningful symbols, or simple words like "Awake" or "Present."

10. **Develop a Rhythm of Retreat**: Schedule regular times—daily, weekly, and seasonally—to step back from activity and cultivate deeper consciousness through extended prayer, meditation, and silence.

The intention is not to add burdensome practices to an already busy life, but to integrate them into a new way of living. The goal is not perfect, uninterrupted consciousness (which is impossible this side of eternity), but a growing capacity to recognize unconsciousness and return to awareness more quickly.

# The Transformative Power of Staying Awake

As you cultivate meditative consciousness, you'll experience transformation in every area of life:

1. **Spiritual Discernment**: You'll more readily distinguish between God's voice, your thoughts, and external influences, leading to more explicit guidance and direction.

2. **Emotional Regulation**: You'll respond to triggers with increasing wisdom and self-control rather than reactive patterns, improving relationships and inner peace.

3. **Mental Clarity**: Your thinking will become more focused and aligned with truth, reducing anxiety and increasing creative problem-solving.

4. **Physical Well-being**: As consciousness extends to bodily awareness, you'll make healthier choices and experience less stress-related illnesses.

5. **Relational Authenticity**: Your interactions will become more present and genuine, characterized by attentive listening and thoughtful responses rather than automatic reactions.

6. **Missional Effectiveness**: You'll notice divine appointments and opportunities that you previously missed, increasing your kingdom's impact.

7. **Worship Depth**: Your awareness of God's presence will transform routine spiritual practices into vibrant encounters with the living God.

These transformations don't happen overnight but emerge gradually as meditative consciousness becomes your more frequent state of being. The journey is not about achieving perfection but about growing awareness and responsiveness to the Spirit's presence and work.

# Choosing Consciousness Moment by Moment

As we conclude this exploration of meditative consciousness versus unconsciousness, remember that the choice between these states presents itself in every moment. Each time you notice that you've drifted into unconsciousness is an opportunity to return to awareness—to "stay awake" as Jesus commanded.

This continuous return to consciousness is the heart of biblical meditation. It's not primarily about designated meditation sessions (though these are valuable) but about cultivating a lifestyle of spiritual wakefulness that permeates every aspect of life.

## CHAPTER THREE:
# The Hebrew Revelation:
## Hagah, Siyach, And Higgayon

To truly understand biblical meditation, we must delve into the original languages of Scripture. The Old Testament, written primarily in Hebrew with some portions in Aramaic, contains rich linguistic treasures that reveal the depth and breadth of meditation as God intended. In this chapter, we will explore three key Hebrew words that translate as "meditate" in English Bibles:

# Hagah (הגה), Siyach (שׂיח) and Higgayon (הגיון)

## Understanding Biblical Hebrew Root Words

Before we examine these specific words, we must comprehend how Hebrew functions as a language. Unlike English, which often requires many words to express complex ideas, Biblical Hebrew uses a system of root words that can convey multiple related meanings. This gives Hebrew an incredible depth and richness that is often lost in translation.

Hebrew root words typically have three consonants, and adding vowels, prefixes, and suffixes to this root creates various word forms. The beauty of this system is that all

[29]

words derived from the same root share a conceptual relationship, revealing connections that might not be immediately obvious to non-Hebrew speakers.

When we study the Hebrew words for meditation, we're not simply looking for direct English equivalents but exploring entire conceptual frameworks that help us understand what meditation truly encompasses according to Scripture. This approach allows us to recover meditation's full, divinely inspired meaning rather than being limited by our modern, often culturally influenced definitions.

# The Multifaceted Nature of Hagah (הגה)

The first and most common Hebrew word translated as "meditate" is Hagah (הגה). This word appears many times throughout the Old Testament and carries a fascinating range of meanings that expand our understanding of meditation far beyond silent contemplation.

According to Strong's Concordance and Hebrew lexicons, Hagah can mean:

1. To moan, growl, utter, muse
2. To speak, declare, or make a sound
3. To ponder, imagine, meditate
4. To plot or devise (often in a negative context)
5. To mutter or murmur (as in reciting to oneself)

This diverse range of meanings reveals Hagah involves internal mental processes and external expressions. It is not merely a silent, passive activity, but can include vocalization, sound, and physical manifestations.

Consider these biblical examples of Hagah in action:

**Isaiah 31:4** states, **"As a lion or a young lion growl (hagah) over its prey." (NKJV)**. The word "Hagah" depicts a lion's low, rumbling growl, full of focused intensity. This usage suggests that meditation can involve a deep, almost primal engagement with its object.

In **Psalm 1:2**, we find the classic meditation verse: **"But his delight is in the law of the LORD, and in His law, he meditates (hagah) day and night." (NKJV)** Here, Hagah refers to the continuous absorption in contemplation of God's Word.

**Psalm 2:1 takes on a different meaning: "Why do the nations rage, and the people plot (hagah) a vain thing?" (NKJV)**

In **Psalm 35:28**, David writes: **"And my tongue shall speak (hagah) of Your righteousness and Your praise all day long." (NKJV)** Here, Hagah involves verbal declaration and praise.

These varied uses of Hagah reveal that biblical meditation is a holistic activity engaging the mind, heart, and voice. It includes pondering deeply, speaking forth, murmuring repeatedly, and even the creative process of forming new thoughts and plans based on what is being meditated upon.

Perhaps most surprisingly, Hagah also means "to purge" or "to clear out dross," suggesting that meditation serves as a cleansing process, removing worthless thoughts and making room for divine truth. This aspect of Hagah aligns perfectly with Paul's instruction to **"take every thought captive to obey Christ"** 2 Corinthians 10:5.

# The Contemplative Power of Siyach (שׂיח)

The second Hebrew word translated as "meditates "is Siyach (שׂיח). This word adds another dimension to our under-standing of biblical meditation, emphasizing communica-tion, conversation, and complaint.

Siyach can mean:

1.  To muse, meditate, consider
2.  To speak, complain, or declare
3.  To commune, converse (with oneself or others)
4.  To pray or talk with God

In **Job 7:11**, we see Siyach used in a complaint: **"Therefore I will not restrain my mouth; I will speak in the anguish of my spirit; I will complain (siyach) in the bitterness of my soul." (KJV)** This usage reveals that biblical meditation can include an honest expression of distress, confusion, or questioning - processing difficult emotions before God.

**Psalm 77:12** uses Siyach in a more positive light: **"I will also meditate (siyach) on all Your work and talk of Your deeds." (KJV)** Here, the word encompasses internal reflection and external verbalization of God's mighty acts.

**Psalm 119:15** combines Siyach with another aspect of meditation: **"I will meditate (siyach) on Your precepts and contemplate Your ways." (NKJV)** This verse suggests a thoughtful consideration of God's instructions and patterns.

These examples reveal that Siyach represents meditation as a dialogue with oneself, others, and God. It portrays meditation not as a monologue or a one-way mental exercise, but as a conversational engagement with divine truth. This dialogical aspect of meditation aligns perfectly with the relational nature of Christianity itself.

# The Resonant Depths of Higgayon (הגיון)

The third Hebrew word in our study is Higgayon (הגיון), which is related to Hagah but carries its distinct nuances. Higgayon appears less frequently in Scripture but adds crucial dimensions to our understanding of biblical meditation.

Higgayon can mean:

1.   Meditation, contemplation

2. Resounding music, solemn sound
3. Whispered musing
4. A meditation set to musical accompaniment

In **Psalm 19:14**, we find the well-known prayer: **"Let the words of my mouth and the meditation (higgayon) of my heart be acceptable in Your sight, O LORD, my strength and my Redeemer." (NKJV)** Higgayon refers to the deep, internal contemplations of the heart that God perceives, even when they are not verbalized.

**Psalm 92:3** uses Higgayon in a musical context: **"On an instrument of ten strings, on the lute, and the harp, with harmonious sound (higgayon)." (NKJV)** This usage connects meditation with musical expression and worship.

**Lamentations 3:62** employs Higgayon to best describe the whispered plots of enemies: **"The lips of my enemies and their whispering (higgayon) against me all day long." (NKJV)** This usage highlights the quiet, continuous nature of certain types of meditation.

What Higgayon adds to our understanding is meditation's rhythmic, musical, and emotional dimensions. Higgayon's work suggests that artistic expression encompassing both actual music and rhythmic thought's internal "music" can enhance meditation. This connection between meditation and music explains why many believers find that worship music facilitates deeper contemplation of God's truth.

# How These Words Transform Our Understanding of Meditation

Combining the insights from these three Hebrew words—Hagah, Siyach, and Higgayon—gives us a revolutionary understanding of biblical meditation.

Far from being limited to silent mental repetition of Scripture, biblical meditation encompasses:

1. **Our entire thought life**: The continuous stream that occupies our minds day and night.

2. **Verbal expression**: Speaking, declaring, complaining, and questioning as part of processing truth.

3. **Creative contemplation**: Actively engaging with truth to form new insights, plans, and applications.

4. **Emotional processing**: Working through feelings, concerns, and reactions in the presence of God.

5. **Artistic and musical engagement**: Using rhythm, melody, and creative expression to internalize and respond to truth.

6. **Dialogical relationship**: Conversing with God, listening, and responding in an ongoing communion.

7. **Purging and cleansing**: Clearing out mental and emotional "dross" to make room for divine truth.

# CHAPTER THREE:
The Hebrew Revelation:
Hagah, Siyach, And Higgayon

This comprehensive view of meditation reveals that we are constantly in a state of meditation—the question is not whether we are meditating, but what we are meditating upon. As Jesus warned in **Matthew 24:42, "Therefore stay awake, for you do not know on what day your Lord is coming." (ESV)** This call to "stay awake" is an exhortation to maintain a conscious awareness of what occupies our meditation.

In the modern world, we constantly face inputs that compete for our mental attention—areas like social media, news, entertainment, advertising, and the opinions of others. Each of these inputs becomes the object of our meditation, shaping our thoughts, emotions, and, ultimately, our actions. Biblical meditation calls us to direct this continuous process toward God's truth intentionally, rather than allowing those worldly influences to capture it.

The Hebrew understanding of meditation also explains why the command to **"meditate day and night"** Joshua 1:8 is not an impossible burden but a recognition of our continuous mental state. We are always in a state of meditation; the spiritual discipline is about consciously directing that state toward God's Word and presence.

# Practical Application:
# Recovering Hebrew Meditation

How can we apply these Hebrew insights to develop a more biblical approach to meditation? Here are some practical steps:

## CHAPTER THREE:
### The Hebrew Revelation:
### Hagah, Siyach, And Higgayon

1. **Recognize your continuous meditative state**: Notice what occupies your thoughts throughout the day. What do you moan about, mutter, or devise in your mind? This awareness is the first step toward redirecting your meditation.

2. **Engage Scripture holistically**: Don't limit yourself to silent reading when meditating on God's Word. Speak it aloud (hagah), converse with God about it (siyach), and express it creatively or musically (higgayon).

3. **Embrace honest dialogue with God**: Following the example of the Psalms, bring your complaints, questions, and struggles into your meditation, allowing God's truth to address them directly.

4. **Incorporate artistic expression**: Consider journaling, drawing, or creating/listening to music as part of your meditation practice, engaging in different aspects of how God designed you.

5. **Practice conscious awareness**: Throughout the day, notice what you're meditating on, gently redirecting your thoughts to God's truth when they wander to unhelpful places.

As we recover these Hebrew dimensions of meditation, we experience the transformative power God intended. Rather than seeing meditation as an isolated spiritual exercise performed at specific times, we should recognize it as the continuous background process of our consciousness that shapes everything else.

In the next chapter, we'll explore how the New Testament builds on this Hebrew foundation through the Greek word Meletao, adding further dimensions to our understanding of biblical meditation. Together, these linguistic insights will provide us with a comprehensive framework for developing a meditation practice that aligns with God's original design— one that engages our whole being and transforms us from the inside out.

# The Hebrew Letters of Hagah:
## Unlocking the Divine Mystery of Meditation

Biblical wisdom holds a profound revelation in its sacred depths, changing how we understand meditation. This revelation isn't merely academic—it's a divine unveiling, carefully hidden within the ancient Hebrew letters, waiting for those with spiritual hunger to discover.

The Hebrew word for meditation, "**Hagah**" (הגה), comprises three letters that form not just a word but a spiritual doorway. Each letter carries cosmic significance, divinely revealing the true essence of communion with God. Let us embark on this sacred journey of discovery, unveiling what God Himself encoded in His holy language.

## The Divine Framework: Heh-Gimel-Heh

The structure of "**Hagah**" (הגה) is truly a marvel of divine architecture. It begins and ends with the same letter —

# Heh (ה)

Creating a sacred envelope that contains the letter **Gimel(ג).** This arrangement mirrors something profoundly significant: the very name of God Himself.

The ineffable name of God:

# YHWH (הוהי)

It contains the letter Heh twice. This is no coincidence. The tetragrammaton—God's most holy name—reveals His eternal nature through its letters:

## "He Was, He Is, He Will Be."

The presence of Heh in both Hagah and YHWH creates an unmistakable connection between meditation and the divine presence.

# Heh (ה): The Breath of God.

Heh is perhaps the most spiritually charged letter in the Hebrew alphabet. It is God's letter, appearing twice in His sacred name. When ancient Hebrew scribes wrote this letter, they understood they were inscribing something of God's essence.

Heh represents:

**BEHOLD!**—A call to spiritual attention and awakening.
**REVELATION**—The unveiling of God's divine mysteries.
**BREATH**—The precious life-giving force that animated Adam.
**SPIRIT**—The divine presence that moves within and around us.
**LIGHT**—The illumination that dispels spiritual darkness.
**DIVINE REVELATION**—God's communication with humanity.
Visually, Heh depicts a person with arms raised toward heaven; the posture of one receiving divine inspiration.

This letter's repetition at the beginning and end of "Hagah" reveals an extraordinary truth: true meditation begins and ends with God's breath and revelation. We enter meditation through divine inspiration and emerge transformed by divine illumination.

# Gimel (ג):
## The Transformative Journey

Gimel stands between these two divine Heh letters—a letter of profound movement and transformation. In ancient pictographic Hebrew, a camel represented Gimel—the desert vessel that carried travelers through harsh landscapes to new destinations.

# Gimel (ג)

Gimel symbolizes:

**JOURNEY**—spiritual pilgrimage and transformation.
**MOVEMENT**—the dynamic flow of spiritual growth.
**PROGRESS** — advancement toward divine understanding.
**NOURISHMENT UNTIL RIPENESS** — the process of spiritual maturation.

This central letter reveals that meditation is not static contemplation, but a transformative journey. The placement of Gimel between two Heh letters shows that our spiritual journey occurs within the protective envelope of God's breath and revelation.

## The Breathtaking Revelation

When we synthesize these letter meanings, we uncover a profound revelation that changes everything we thought we knew about biblical meditation:

**"Behold, The Spirit/Breath of God Moves Through Us and Reveals His Divine Spiritual Light as We Travel Through Our Daily Lives."**

[41]

This is not merely an intellectual insight—it's a cosmic unveiling of God's design for human-divine communion. According to the Creator Himself, meditation is the pathway through which His breath flows into our being, transforming our consciousness as we journey through life.

The presence of **"breath"** in the meaning of Heh illuminates why breathing awareness is the foundation of Christian meditation. Each conscious breath we take activates the divine meaning encoded in Hagah—opening us to receive God's revelation and allowing His Spirit to move within us.

# The Divine Pattern Revealed

The structure of "Hagah" mirrors the divine name—**YHWH**—with the letter Heh appearing in crucial positions. Just as God's name reveals His eternal nature across all time (past, present, future), the word Hagah reveals the eternal pathway of divine connection. Through the breath, we enter a meditative consciousness that transcends time and allows us to experience God's presence throughout our daily journey.

This revelation transforms meditation from a mere practice into a divine encounter—a sacred pathway designed by God Himself and encoded in the very letters of His holy language. Through this understanding, we don't just practice meditation; we take part in a divine mystery established before the foundation of the world.

As we embrace this profound revelation, we understand why the Psalmist declared that meditation on God's word brings prosperity and fruitfulness. It's not merely about mental focus—it's about activating the divine design encoded in the Hebrew letters themselves, allowing God's breath to flow through us, transforming our consciousness and daily experience into a living testimony of His presence.

# CHAPTER FOUR:
# The Greek Insight: Meletao

While the Hebrew words of the Old Testament provide a rich foundation for understanding biblical meditation, the New Testament adds another crucial dimension through Greek. As we transition from the Hebrew Scriptures to the Greek New Testament, we indeed discover how early Christians understood and practiced meditation in light of Christ's coming and the indwelling of the Holy Spirit.

## The New Testament Perspective

They wrote the New Testament in Koine Greek, the common language of the Mediterranean world during Jesus's time and the early church. This linguistic shift from Hebrew to Greek reflects the expansion of God's message beyond Israel to all nations. Just as the gospel message spread across cultural boundaries, the concept of meditation also took on new dimensions while maintaining its essential spiritual purpose.

In the New Testament, the primary Greek word translated as "meditate" is **Meletao (μελετάω)**. Though it appears less frequently than its Hebrew counterparts in the Old Testament, Meletao carries significant weight in understanding how meditation developed in Christian practice after Christ's resurrection and the coming of the Holy Spirit.

# Meletao (μελετάω): To Care for and Attend Carefully

According to Greek lexicons and Strong's Concordance, Meletao encompasses several related meanings:

1.  **To care for, attend to carefully.**
2.  **To practice, exercise, and train oneself.**
3.  **To revolve in the mind, ponder.**
4.  **To imagine, premeditate.**
5.  **To study diligently.**

The most striking aspect of Meletao is its emphasis on careful attention and practice. Unlike some passive conceptions of meditation, Meletao portrays meditation as an active, intentional discipline that requires effort and engagement.

In **1 Timothy 4:15**, Paul instructs young Timothy: **"Meditate (meletao) on these things; give yourself entirely to them, that your progress may be evident to all." (NKJV)**

The context of this verse is Paul's exhortation to Timothy regarding his spiritual gifts and ministerial responsibilities. Using Meletao, Paul shows that meditation is not merely contemplative but transformative—it should produce visible progress and growth.

This usage reveals that New Testament meditation is deeply practical. It's not about achieving some mystical state, but about allowing God's truth to reshape our character, abilities, and actions in ways others can observe. The phrase "give yourself entirely to them" emphasizes total commitment to this process of meditation and transformation.

Another significant example of "Meletao" appears in Acts 4:25, which quotes Psalm 2:1: **"Why do the nations rage, and the peoples Devise (meletao) futile things?" (NKJV)**

# Active vs. Passive Meditation

The Greek concept of Meletao helps us distinguish between active and passive approaches to meditation. Many modern forms of meditation emphasize emptying the mind or achieving a state of detached awareness. These approaches are passive, focusing on the cessation of mental activity.

In contrast, as expressed through Meletao, biblical meditation actively engages with its object. Rather than emptying the mind, it fills the mind with God's truth. Rather than detaching from thoughts, it attaches deeply to specific thoughts—God's thoughts as revealed in Scripture. Rather than seeking a state of non-doing, it seeks transformation that leads to purposeful action.

This active nature of biblical meditation aligns with Jesus' teaching that the truth will set us free (John 8:32). Freedom comes not from escaping reality through passive meditation but from engaging deeply with divine truth through active meditation, allowing it to transform our perception, under-standing, and response to reality.

The Greek word Meletao also conveys practice and training, as an athlete or musician would practice their craft. This suggests that meditation is a skill that improves with consistent application. Just as a pianist becomes more proficient through daily practice, a believer becomes more adept at meditation through regular exercise of this spiritual discipline.

# Stirring the Gifts Through Meditation

One of the most potent aspects of Meletao is its connection with the activation of spiritual gifts. In **1 Timothy 4:14-15**, Paul writes: **"Do not neglect the gift that is in you, which was given to you by prophecy with the laying on of the hands of the eldership. Meditate (meletao) on these things; give yourself entirely to them, that your progress may be evident to all." (NKJV)**

This passage reveals that meditation stirs up and develops the spiritual gifts God has placed within us. We activate and strengthen these divine endowments through intentional, focused meditation on God's truth and our calling.

This concept adds a truly dynamic dimension to our understanding of meditation. It's not merely about reflecting on Scripture in an abstract sense, but about allowing that reflection to activate the spiritual potential God has placed within all of us. Meditation becomes a catalyst for the manifestation of God's gifts in our lives.

The phrase "that your progress may be manifest to all" shows that this type of meditation produces visible results. As we meditate on God's Word and our spiritual calling, others should be able to observe our growth and development. This external evidence confirms that our meditation practice is authentic and engaging.

# Practical Application:
## Implementing Meletao in Your Life

How can we apply the Greek concept of meletao to develop a more effective meditation practice? Here are some practical steps:

1. **Approach meditation as active training.** Rather than seeing meditation as a passive relaxation technique, approach it as spiritual training that requires focus, effort, and consistency.

2. **Meditate with purpose**: Identify specific areas of your spiritual life that need development and direct your meditation toward those areas. For example, if you struggle with patience, meditate on Scriptures that address patience, focusing on the specific growth goal in that area.

3. **Give yourself entirely to it**: Set aside dedicated time for undistracted meditation, giving it your full attention rather than treating it as a background activity.

4. **Look for evidence of progress**: Regularly assess whether your meditation practice produces visible growth in your character, spiritual gifts, and effectiveness in ministry.

5. **Practice spiritual gift activation**: During meditation, consciously focus on the spiritual gifts God has given you, asking the Holy Spirit to activate and strengthen them through your meditation.

6. **Combine contemplation with action**: Allow your meditation to flow naturally into an application, putting into practice the insights and directives you receive during meditation.

By incorporating these elements of Meletao into our meditation practice, we align ourselves more closely with the New Testament understanding of this vital spiritual discipline.

# Bridging Hebrew and Greek Concepts

When we combine the Hebrew concepts of Hagah, Siyach, and Higgayon with the Greek idea of Meletao, a comprehensive picture of biblical meditation emerges. The Hebrew words emphasize meditation's continuous, expressive, and creative aspects, while the Greek word highlights its careful attention, practice, and transformative purpose.

Together, these linguistic insights reveal that biblical meditation is:

1. **Continuous:** A moment-by-moment state of consciousness that encompasses our entire thought life.
2. **Expressive**: Involving not just silent contemplation but also verbalization, conversation, and creative expression.

3. **Attentive**: Requiring careful focus and deliberate engagement with divine truth.
4. **Practical:** aimed at transformation and the development of spiritual gifts.
5. **Progressive**: Designed to produce visible growth and advancement in our spiritual journey.
6. **Holistic**: Engaging our entire being—mind, emotions, voice, and actions.

This comprehensive understanding of meditation starkly contrasts the simplified Christian notion of "revolving a Bible verse in your mind" and the Eastern concept of emptying the mind or detaching from thought. Biblical meditation is richer, more dynamic, and more transformative than these limited conceptions.

# The Role of the Holy Spirit in Meditation

A crucial aspect of the New Testament meditation that distinguishes it from traditional Old Testament practice is the indwelling presence of the Holy Spirit. Jesus promises that the Holy Spirit will **"teach you all things and bring to your remembrance all things that I said to you." John 14:26** and would **"guide you into all truth." John 16:13 (NKJV)**

Christian meditation is not a solitary mental exercise, but a collaborative engagement with the divine teacher who dwells within us. As we meditate on Scripture, the Holy Spirit illuminates our understanding, applies truth to our specific circumstances, and empowers us to respond appropriately.

The Greek concept of meletao, emphasizing careful attention and practice, aligns perfectly with this collaborative relationship. We attend carefully to the written Word and the internal guidance of the Spirit, practicing what we learn under His tutelage.

This partnership with the Holy Spirit transforms meditation from a discipline we perform in our strength to a supernatural encounter that transcends our natural capabilities. Meditation becomes informative, revelatory, reflective, prophetic, disciplinary, and empowering through the Spirit's involvement.

# Conclusion: The Transformative Power of Meletao

As we conclude our exploration of the Greek concept of meletao, we recognize that New Testament meditation offers a powerful pathway to spiritual transformation. By attending carefully to God's truth, practicing its application in our lives, and allowing it to activate our spiritual gifts, we position ourselves for visible, progressive growth in our Christian journey.

The Greek insight into meditation complements and expands upon the Hebrew foundation, providing a complete picture of how God intended this spiritual discipline to function in the lives of His people. Together, these linguistic treasures restore meditation's complete, biblical understanding, partially lost in modern Christian practice.

# CHAPTER FOUR:
## The Greek Insight: Meletao

In the next chapter, we'll explore how modern science has confirmed what Scripture has taught about meditation's transformative power. We'll discover how recent research on neuroplasticity, stress reduction, and cognitive function aligns with biblical principles and provides additional motivation for developing a consistent meditation practice.

# CHAPTER FIVE:
# The Science of Spiritual Meditation

In recent decades, science has caught up with what the Bible has taught for millennia about the power of meditation. As researchers explore the effects of various meditation practices on the brain, body, and overall well-being, they discover evidence confirming God's command to meditate on His Lord Day and night. In this chapter, we'll explore the fascinating intersection of modern scientific research and ancient biblical practice, revealing how science affirms the transformative power of meditation.

## Modern Research on Meditation and the Brain

Neuroscience has made remarkable discoveries about how meditation affects the brain. Using advanced imaging technologies like functional magnetic resonance imaging (fMRI) and electroencephalography (EEG), researchers have documented significant changes in brain structure and function among regular meditators.

One of the most striking findings is that meditation changes the physical structure of the brain—a phenomenon known as neuroplasticity. Studies have shown that regular meditation increases gray matter density in brain regions associated with attention, emotional regulation, and self-awareness. It also strengthens connections between different brain regions, improving communication and integration.

[53]

CHAPTER FIVE:
The Science of Spiritual Meditation

Dr. Andrew Newberg, a neuroscientist who has extensively studied the brain during spiritual practices, explains: "When people engage in prayer or meditation, we observe increased activity in the frontal lobes—areas associated with attention and concentration—and decreased activity in the parietal lobes, which orient us in space and time. This neural pattern correlates with reports of transcendent experiences, feelings of connection with something greater than oneself, and a sense of timelessness."

These findings align perfectly with the biblical concept of meditation as an engaged, attentive practice (Meletao) that connects us with eternal realities beyond our immediate physical circumstances. When Scripture calls us to **"set your minds on things above, not on earthly things." Colossians 3:2 (NIV)** prescribes a practice that science confirms can reshape our brains.

# Neuroplasticity and Spiritual Formation

Neuroplasticity—the brain's ability to reorganize itself by forming new neural connections—provides a scientific framework for understanding how meditation contributes to spiritual transformation. The apostle Paul urges believers to transform themselves by renewing their minds (Romans 12:2), a statement that our current understanding of neuroplasticity gives new significance.

When we repeatedly focus on God's truth through meditation, we strengthen neural pathways associated with those thoughts and weaken pathways associated with contrary patterns. Over time, this process rewires our brains, making godly thoughts and responses more automatic and ungodly ones less dominant.

Dr. Caroline Leaf, a cognitive neuroscientist and Christian author, explains: "Every time you think, you build a thought. Every time you build a thought, you're changing the physical structure of your brain." This scientific insight helps us understand why God commands Joshua to meditate on the law/Instructions/directions/guidance all **"day and night" (Joshua 1:8)**—the consistency creates lasting neural changes that transform our default thinking patterns.

Research has shown that even short periods of regular meditation (8-12 weeks) can produce measurable changes in brain structure. Imagine the profound neural transformation that occurs through years of consistent biblical meditation! Therefore, long-term meditators often report that Scripture has become so internalized that it spontaneously comes to mind in relevant situations—they have physically rewired their brains around God's Word.

# The Body-Mind-Spirit Connection

Biblical anthropology has consistently recognized human beings' integrated nature as the body (soul, mind, will, emotions), and spirit. Modern science confirms this holistic understanding by documenting the intricate connections between physical, mental, and spiritual well-being.

CHAPTER FIVE:
The Science of Spiritual Meditation

Research has shown that meditation affects not only the brain but also many bodily systems:

1.  **Immune System**: Studies show that regular meditation boosts immune function, increasing antibody production and enhancing the activity of natural killer cells that fight viruses and cancer.

2.  **Cardiovascular System**: Meditation reduces blood pressure, heart rate, and stress hormones like cortisol and adrenaline, decreasing the risk of heart disease and stroke.

3.  **Endocrine System**: Meditation helps us regulate the hormones related to stress, sleep, mood, and metabolism, promoting overall hormonal balance.

4.  **Respiratory System**: Controlled breathing, often associated with meditation, improves lung function, oxygen utilization, and respiratory efficiency.

These physiological benefits align with biblical promises about the health benefits of spiritual practices. **Proverbs 3:7-8** advice, **"Do not be wise in your own eyes; fear the LORD and shun evil. This will bring health to your body and nourishment to your bones." (NKJV)** Similarly, **Proverbs 17:22** observes, **"A cheerful heart is excellent medicine, but a crushed spirit dries up the bones."**

The Hebrew shalom (Peace) concept — complete well-being in body, mind, relationships, and spirit—reflects this integrated understanding. Biblical meditation contributes to shalom by aligning our entire being with God's design and purposes.

# Scientific Evidence for Meditation's Benefits

Beyond the general findings about brain structure and bodily systems, specific research studies have documented many benefits of regular meditation practice:

1. **Stress Reduction**: Multiple studies have shown that meditation activates the parasympathetic nervous system (the "rest and digest" response) while reducing activity in the sympathetic nervous system (the "fight or flight" response). This shift helps the body recover from stress and prevents chronic stress-related conditions.

2. **Improved Attention and Concentration:** Research at the University of Wisconsin found that meditation training increased participants' ability to sustain attention and filter out distractions. This enhanced focus aligns with the biblical concept of **"fixing our eyes"** on Jesus **(Hebrews 12:2)** and **"setting our minds on things above" (Colossians 3:2).**

3. **Enhanced Emotional Regulation**: Studies have shown that regular meditators show greater activation in brain regions associated with emotional regulation and reduced activity in the amygdala, which processes fear and anxiety. This scientific finding corresponds with biblical promises about **"the peace of God, which transcends all understanding" (Philippians 4:7).**

[57]

4.  **Increased Compassion and Empathy**: Research at Emory University found that meditation practices focused on compassion increased altruistic behavior and empathic responses to others' suffering. This aligns with biblical commands to "**love your neighbor as yourself**" **(Mark 12:31) and "clothe yourselves with compassion, kindness, humility, gentleness and patience" (Colossians 3:12)**.

5.  **Reduced Symptoms of Depression and Anxiety:** Multiple clinical trials have shown that meditation-based interventions can significantly reduce symptoms of depression and anxiety, sometimes as effective as medication. This supports the biblical promise that "**God has not given us a spirit of fear but of power, love, and a sound mind**" **2 Timothy 1:7**.

6.  **Improved Sleep Quality**: Research published in JAMA Internal Medicine found that mindfulness meditation improved sleep quality in adults with sleep disturbances. This benefit connects with the biblical theme of rest, exemplified in **Psalm 4:8: "In peace, I will lie down and sleep, for you alone, LORD, make me dwell in safety."**

7.  **Enhanced Immune Function**: Studies at the University of Wisconsin and Harvard Medical School have documented improved immune responses in meditators, including increased antibody production in response to vaccines and enhanced activity of natural killer cells. This scientific finding gives new meaning to the

biblical promise that **"the prayer offered in faith will make the sick person well" (James 5:15).**

These research findings validate biblical meditation as a legitimate practice and provide additional motivation for incorporating it into our daily lives. God's commands are always for our benefit, and science confirms the wisdom of His instruction to meditate on His Word.

# How Science Confirms Biblical Wisdom

The convergence of scientific research and biblical teaching on meditation reveals several essential principles:

1. **God's Commands Are Biologically Wise**: When God instructed His people to meditate on His Lord Day and night, He wasn't imposing an arbitrary spiritual discipline. He prescribed a practice that He, as our Creator, knew would optimize our brain function, reduce stress, improve health, and enhance well-being.

2. **Transformation Is Both Spiritual and Neurological**: The biblical concept of renewing the mind (Romans 12:2) has a neurological component. Meditating on God's truth allows the Holy Spirit to work through the brain's natural plasticity, literally rewiring our neural pathways so that godly thoughts and responses become more automatic.

3. **Consistency Is Key**: Both Scripture and science emphasize the importance of regular, consistent

meditation. **Joshua 1:8** prescribes meditation **"day and night,"** and neuroscience confirms that lasting brain changes require repetition and consistency.

4. **Holistic Integration Is God's Design**: The scientific evidence for the amazing mind-body-spirit connection confirms the biblical anthropology of humans as integrated beings. When we meditate on God's Word, the benefits extend beyond our spiritual life to our mental and physical well-being.

5. **Different Meditation Have Different Effects**: Research has shown that different meditation practices activate different brain regions and produce different effects. This aligns with the biblical presentation of various types of meditation (as seen in the Hebrew words Hagah, Siyach, and Higgayon), each serving different spiritual purposes.

It's important to note that while scientific research on meditation often focuses on secular or Eastern practices, the principles also apply to biblical meditation. Christian meditation may offer unique benefits because it combines the neurological benefits of focused attention with the spiritual power of engaging with divine truth and the indwelling Holy Spirit.

# Practical Application: Science Informed Biblical Meditation

How can we apply these scientific insights to enhance our biblical meditation practice? Here are some practical suggestions:

1. **Consistency Over Duration**: Research suggests that regular, brief meditation sessions (even 10-15 minutes daily) produce more significant brain changes than occasional longer meditation sessions. This makes biblical meditation accessible even for busy people; consistent daily practice is more important than lengthy sessions.

2. **Engage Multiple Brain Systems**: Incorporate various aspects of biblical meditation (Hagah, Siyach, Higgayon, and Meletao) to activate different brain regions. Speak Scripture aloud, write it down, sing it, visualize it, and discuss it with others to create richer neural connections.

3. **Use Breath Awareness**: Research has shown that controlled breathing enhances meditation's effects on the nervous system. Begin meditation with slow breathing to activate the parasympathetic nervous system and prepare your brain for deeper engagement with God's Word.

4. **Create Environmental Cues**: Neuroscience research on habit formation suggests that environmental cues help establish consistent practices. Designate a specific

place for meditation and use consistent sensory cues (like a particular candle, music, or posture) to signal your brain that it's time to enter a meditative state.

5. **Leverage Peak Neuroplasticity Times**: Research has shown that the brain is receptive to forming new neural pathways during the first 30 minutes after waking and the last 30 minutes before sleep. These times align perfectly with the recommended instructions for the best meditating times.

6. **Practice Progressive Training**: Just as physical exercise requires progressive overload for continued development, meditation benefits from gradually increasing challenges. Begin with shorter, simpler meditation practices and progressively extend your duration and depth.

7. **Monitor Tangible Outcomes**: Research studies use measurable outcomes to assess meditation's effectiveness. Similarly, look for concrete evidence of your meditation's impact—improved emotional regulation, enhanced focus, greater peace, increased compassion, and other fruits of the Spirit (Galatians 5:22-23).

Integrating these science-informed approaches with biblical principles allows us to develop a meditation practice that honors God while maximizing the neurological and physiological benefits He designed into this spiritual discipline.

# Conclusion: The Harmony of Science and Scripture

As we conclude our exploration of the science of spiritual meditation, we recognize the beautiful harmony between modern research and ancient biblical wisdom. Science isn't discovering new truths about meditation; it's confirming what God has revealed in His Word.

This convergence shouldn't surprise us. The God who created the human brain and established the laws of neuroplasticity is the same God who prescribed meditation as a spiritual discipline. His commands align with His design.

The scientific evidence for meditation benefits provides additional motivation for obedience to God's instruction. When we understand that meditation not only pleases God but also optimizes our brain function, reduces stress, improves health, and enhances well-being, we're more likely to prioritize this practice in our busy lives.

As we move forward in our exploration of biblical meditation, let's carry these scientific insights with us, recognizing that when we meditate on God's Word, we're not just engaging in a spiritual exercise — we're taking part in a process that transforms us at every level: spirit, soul, and body. This holistic transformation is what Paul described as being **"transformed by the renewing of your mind" (Romans 12:2)**.

In the next chapter, we'll explore the biblical concept of the breath of life and its connection to the Holy Spirit, exploring

# CHAPTER FIVE:
## The Science of Spiritual Meditation

how conscious breathing can enhance our meditation practice and deepen our spiritual connection with God.

# CHAPTER SIX:
# The Divine Mystery
## Of God's Breath of Life

When God created the heavens and the earth, breathing was one of His first recorded actions. **Genesis 1:2** tells us that **"the Spirit of God was hovering over the waters,"** and the **Hebrew word for Spirit—Ruach—also means "breath" or "wind**." This divine breath was present at creation, infusing life and order into the formless void. Later, in **Genesis 2:7,** we read that **"the LORD God formed man of the dust of the ground and breathed into his nostrils the breath of life; and man became a living soul." (KJV)**

These passages reveal a profound truth that will transform your understanding of meditation: the breath filling your lungs right now is not merely a biological function, but a sacred connection to your Creator. The very air you're breathing carries the divine imprint established at creation. This chapter explores the biblical revelation of breath through three interconnected concepts—the Hebrew words Ruach and Neshama and the Greek word Pneuma—and their profound implications for your meditation practice and spiritual growth.

CHAPTER SIX:
The Divine Mystery
Of God's Breath of Life

# The Divine Breath in Scripture: A Progressive Revelation

Scripture presents a progressive revelation of the divine breath, beginning with creation and culminating in the indwelling presence of the Holy Spirit in believers. Scripture uses three key terms to describe this divine breath, progressively revealing deeper dimensions of your connection to God through breathing.

# RUACH (רוּחַ):

The foundational Hebrew term that connects breath, wind, and spirit.

# NESHAMA (נְשָׁמָה):

The text explicitly gives the specialized Hebrew term for the divine breath to humans.

# PNEUMA (πνεῦμα):

The Greek term that fulfills and expands these concepts in the New Testament.

Together, these terms reveal a comprehensive theology of breath that transforms your understanding of meditation. Let's explore each concept and how they build upon one another to enrich your spiritual practice.

# The Hebrew Word "Ruach "(רוּ"):
# The Foundation of Divine Breath

To fully understand the biblical concept of breath, you must begin with the rich meanings of the Hebrew word **"Ruach"** (רוּחַ). The Old Testament uses this multifaceted term nearly 400 times, translating it as "spirit," "breath," "wind," or "mind" depending on the context.

The semantic range of Ruach reveals the interconnectedness of concepts that you might often separate in modern thinking:

1.  **Physical Breath:** In its most basic sense, Ruach refers to the physical act of breathing. **Ecclesiastes 3:19** notes that humans and animals have the same Ruach, referring to the breath that sustains physical life.

2.  **Wind or Air in Motion:** Ruach also describes the movement of air in the natural world. **Genesis 8:1** tells us God made **"Ruach to pass over the earth, and the waters subsided,"** referring to the wind that dried the flood waters.

3.  **Life Force or Vitality**: Beyond mere respiration, Ruach represents the animating force that gives energy and vitality. A crushed or faint spirit (Ruach) leaves you lacking energy and motivation.

4.  **Emotional or Mental State**: Ruach can refer to your emotional or mental disposition. **Proverbs 16:18** warns

that "**pride goes before destruction, a haughty Ruach before a fall,**" referring to an attitude or state of mind.

5. **The Human Spirit**: Ruach often designates the immaterial part of your being that relates to God. **Zechariah 12:1** describes God as the one **"who forms the Ruach of man within him."**

6. **Divine Spirit**: Ruach refers to God's Spirit. **Isaiah 61:1** proclaims, **"The Ruach of the Lord GOD is upon me,"** referring to the divine presence and power.

This linguistic connection between breath, wind, human spirit, and the Divine Spirit is not coincidental. It reveals God's design for you—you're breathing constantly reminds you of your spiritual nature and divine connection. Every breath you take can serve as a moment of communion with God's Ruach.

# The Hidden Revelation in the Hebrew Letters of Ruach

Have you ever considered that God might have encoded spiritual treasures within the very letters of the Hebrew alphabet? When you look beyond the meaning of Ruach, you'll discover an even more profound revelation hidden within the three Hebrew letters that form this sacred word.

Take a moment to breathe deeply as you consider each letter of **Ruach (רוּחַ)** and what God might reveal to you through them. Here is the first one:

# Resh (ר)

The first letter you encounter in Ruach **Resh** represents the **"Holiness of God."** As you breathe in, imagine drawing on this divine holiness. This initial letter reminds you that your breath originates from God's holy nature. With each inhalation, you are not merely taking in oxygen—you're receiving something that carries God's holiness into your being.

# Vav (ו)

The middle letter **Vav** represents **"Connection with Heaven and Earth."** as you continue breathing, feel how this letter serves as a bridge in your experience. In Hebrew, Vav often functions as a connector, joining words and concepts. Similarly, in your breathing, this letter symbolizes how your breath connects your physical existence with spiritual reality. Each breath you take simultaneously grounds you on Earth while connecting you to heaven.

# Cheth (ח)

The final letter **Cheth** represents **"Binding with God."** As you complete your breath cycle, recognize how this letter emphasizes the covenant relationship established through breathing. Each inhalation and exhalation you experience reinforces your sacred bond with the Creator. Your breathing is a biological function and a continuous renewal of your connection with God.

When you bring these letter meanings together in your meditation, they reveal a powerful declaration that God is speaking over you:

## "Within The Breath Flows the Holiness of God, Who Binds and Connects Us To Heaven And Earth."

Isn't it amazing to think that with every breath you've ever taken, God has been communicating this truth to you? Your breathing carries God's Holiness into your being, connecting you simultaneously to both physical and spiritual realms, reinforcing your covenant relationship with God, and providing you with a constant opportunity for divine communion.

The next time you focus on your breath during meditation, remember that you're not merely performing a relaxation technique; you're reconnecting with the divine gift that animates your being, carries God's holiness, and facilitates your communion with Heaven and Earth.

## The Hebrew Word "Neshama" (נְשָׁמָה): The Specialized Divine Breath

While Ruach encompasses the broader concept of breath and spirit in Hebrew thought, God has also revealed a more specific term—Neshama—that provides deeper insight into the unique breath He gave specifically to you as a human being. This specialized term builds upon your understanding of Ruach and reveals the intimate connection between your physical breathing and God's spiritual presence.

Your journey into this divine mystery begins at creation itself, where you witness the most intimate moment between the Creator and the created:

**"And the Lord God formed man of the dust of the ground and breathed (NAPHACH) into his nostrils the Breath (NESHAMA) of Life, and man became a living being." Genesis 2:7(NKJV)**

This is not merely a historical account, but a divine revelation of your spiritual origin. The Hebrew word "Neshama" reveals that what God breathed into Adam was not simply oxygen, but His essence. The first human breath was divine. The implications for you are staggering: the substance that animates your physical body carries the imprint of God's nature.

Unlike other aspects of creation that came into being through God's spoken word ("Let there be..."), you, as a human being, received God's direct, intimate breath. This divine in-breathing established a sacred connection between your human breath and God's divine presence that continues today.

This revelation deepens as you explore the testimony of Job, who declares:

# CHAPTER SIX:
## The Divine Mystery
## Of God's Breath of Life

## "The Spirit (Ruach) of God has made me, and the Breath (Neshama) of the Almighty gives me life." Job 33:4(NKJV)

Did you notice the present tense — **"gives me life"**? This is not a one-time creation event, but an ongoing, moment-by-moment sustenance in your life. The divine breath that first animated Adam continues to flow through you, sustaining your very existence.

Even more revealing—and utterly shocking—is Job's profound declaration:

## "As long as my Breath (RUACH/SPIRITUAL) is in me and the Spirit of God (NESHAMA/BREATH) IS IN MY NOSTRILS, my lips will not speak wickedness, and my tongue will not utter deceit." Job 27:3-4(NKJV)

Stop and let the magnitude of this revelation sink in! This is not merely poetic language—it's a stunning disclosure of spiritual reality that should leave you breathless. Job reveals something so profound that it changes how you understand your connection to God. He asserts an intimate connection between God's spiritual breath, your spirit, and your breath.

Take a moment and experience this for yourself. Place your hand near your nose and feel the air draw into your nostrils as you inhale. That breath-the very one you just felt—contains the divine essence of God Himself! This isn't metaphorical; it's literal. With every inhalation, you're drawing in oxygen and the living presence of the Almighty Creator.

Can you grasp how revolutionary this understanding is? The boundary between you and God is thinner than you ever imagined. His spiritual essence flows into your physical body with every breath you take. This means that when you seek God for wisdom, understanding, knowledge, and strength against your sinful nature, you can do so by simply focusing on the breath of life that's already flowing through you.

And if that weren't astonishing enough, Scripture reveals even more about what this divine Ruach provides for you as a believer:

**"The Spirit (Ruach) of the LORD will rest on him—the Spirit (Ruach) of WISDOM and UNDERSTANDING, the Spirit (Ruach) of COUNSEL and of MIGHT, the Spirit (Ruach) of the KNOWLEDGE and FEAR of the LORD,"
Isaiah 11:2**

This verse unveils the supernatural benefits that flow through the Ruach. The same breath/spirit connection you experience provides you with Divine wisdom to navigate life's complexities, a Supernatural understanding of spiritual truths, heavenly counsel for difficult decisions, mighty power to overcome your sinful nature, intimate knowledge of God Himself, and proper reverence and awe of the Lord.

The Ruach, which you now understand as both the Spirit and the Breath of God, is the supernatural fuel to strengthen your spiritual walk with God. This revelation transforms your understanding of what it means to be "filled with the Spirit." It's a theological concept and a practical, physical reality you can experience with every conscious breath.

This understanding gives a new dimension to many biblical verses about being filled by the Spirit. When Scripture instructs you to be **"filled with the Spirit" (Ephesians 5:18)**, it invites conscious engagement with and awareness of the divine breath already flowing through your nostrils—the essence of God Himself.

# The Sacred Mystery in the Hebrew Letters of Neshama

# Neshama (נְשָׁמָה)

Just as you discovered with Ruach, the Hebrew word contains an even more profound revelation when you examine the individual letters that compose it. Each of the four Hebrew letters unveils a specific aspect of the divine breath God imparted uniquely to you.

Take another deep breath and let God reveal to you the spiritual treasures hidden within each letter of Neshama: The first one we come across is **Nun**.

# Nun (נ)

As you breathe in, connect with this first letter representing:

**Emergence–Faith**.

Feel how your divine breath brings forth faith and spiritual emergence within you. Your breathing intimately connects your spiritual growth and development of trust in God. With each breath, you can strengthen your faith and fully emerge into your spiritual identity.

# Shin (ש)

As you inhale again, experience this second letter. **Shin** representing

**Wholeness, Peace, and Harmony with God.**

This letter visually resembles flames, suggesting that your breath brings spiritual wholeness and shalom (peace) in all dimensions of your life. Your conscious breathing facilitates harmony with God's presence, integrating your fragmented parts.

# Mem(מ)

As you complete your inhalation, receive this third letter, Mem, which represents:

## Revealed Knowledge of God—Lovingkindness of God.

This letter symbolizes water in Hebrew thought, connecting your breath to divine revelation and God's lovingkindness (chesed). Your breathing can facilitate spiritual insight and understanding of God's nature, washing over you with holy compassion.

# Heh (ה)

As you exhale, express this last letter **heh**, representing

## Behold, Reveal, Breathe, God's presence, and Existence in the Light.

This letter, part of God's sacred name, YHWH, directly connects your breathing to the divine presence. Your breath reveals God's existence and light in your life, making the invisible God tangible in your experience.

Bringing these letter meanings together in meditation reveals an extraordinary declaration that God is speaking into your life:

**"Behold! The emergence of God's Breath of life reveals His presence, faith, knowledge, lovingkindness, peace, wholeness, and existence in the light."**

Isn't it wonderful to discover that breathing strengthens your faith, brings wholeness, peace, and harmony with God, carries divine knowledge and lovingkindness into your experience, and reveals God's presence and light in your daily existence?

The concept of Neshama adds a crucial dimension to your understanding of Ruach. While Ruach applies to all living creatures and various manifestations of breath and spirit, Neshama refers explicitly to the divine breath that makes you unique among creation. This specialized breath carries the divine image and enables you to have spiritual communion with God in ways that other creatures cannot.

# The Greek Word "Pneuma" (πνεῦμα): The Fulfillment in Christ

The divine revelation of breath doesn't end with the Old Testament Hebrew concepts. In the Greek New Testament, the word **"Pneuma" (πνεῦμα)** fulfills and expands this revelation. Like its Hebrew counterparts, Pneuma encompasses multiple related meanings that build upon the foundation established by Ruach and Neshama.

Pneuma appears 385 times across 350 verses in the New Testament and carries these interconnected meanings that deepen your understanding:

# CHAPTER SIX:
## The Divine Mystery
## Of God's Breath of Life

1.  **Breath or Wind:** In its basic sense, Pneuma refers to moving air, whether breath or wind. In **John 3:8,** Jesus uses this meaning in a wordplay that speaks directly to your experience: **"The wind (pneuma) blows where it wishes, and you hear its sound, but you do not know where it comes from or goes. So it is with everyone born of the Spirit (pneuma)."**

2.  **Life Principle**: Pneuma can designate the animating force that gives life to your body. **James 2:26** states that **"the body apart from the Spirit (pneuma) is dead,"** referring to this life-giving principle.

3.  **The Human Spirit**: Pneuma often refers to your human spirit, the immaterial part of you that can commune with God. Paul prays in **1 Thessalonians 5:23 that "your whole Spirit (pneuma) and soul and body be kept blameless."**

4.  **The Holy Spirit**: Most prominently in the New Testament, Pneuma refers to the Holy Spirit, the third person of the Trinity who now dwells within you as a believer. **Acts 2:4** describes how **"they were all filled with the Holy Spirit (Pneuma) and began to speak in other tongues as the Spirit (Pneuma) gave them utterance."**

5.  **Spiritual Realities**: Pneuma can also refer to spiritual beings or realities that influence your life, whether divine or demonic. **1 John 4:1** advises you to

The Divine Mystery
Of God's Breath of Life

**"not believe every Spirit (pneuma) but test the
Spirits (pneuma) to see whether they are from God."**

The Greek concept of Pneuma fulfills and expands your
understanding of divine breath in several important ways:

Consider the profound moment when Jesus, after His
resurrection, imparts the Holy Spirit to His disciples—and by
extension, to you:

**"Again, Jesus says, Peace be with you! As the Father has sent
me, I am sending you. And with that, he breathed on them
and said, Receive the Holy Spirit." John 20:21-22(NIV)**

Have you ever wondered why Jesus chose to breathe on them
rather than lay hands on them or anoint them with oil? This
was no arbitrary gesture, but a deliberate fulfillment of the
divine truth established in Genesis: the breath is the vehicle
of the Spirit. Jesus was consciously reenacting God's breathing
into Adam, symbolizing the new creation and life that comes
through the Spirit—a new creation that includes you.

This revelation reaches its climax at Pentecost, which
establishes a pattern for your own spiritual experience:

**"And suddenly, there came from Heaven a sound like a
mighty rushing wind (Pneuma), and it filled the entire
house where they were sitting... And they were all filled
with the Holy Spirit." — Acts 2:2-4 (ESV)**

The Holy Spirit manifested as a mighty wind—the divine
breath filling the room—and the disciples received this power

[79]

by breathing it in. The pattern established at creation continues in your life: God's Spirit flows into you through the breath.

While Ruach established your connection between breath and spirit, and Neshama revealed the unique divine breath given to you as a human, Pneuma completes this revelation by showing that through Christ, the Holy Spirit now dwells within you, making your body a temple of God's presence **(1 Corinthians 6:19).**

This indwelling presence transforms your understanding of breath in meditation. When you focus on your breath during Christian meditation, you're not just connecting with a divine gift (as in the Old Testament) but engaging with the actual presence of God within you. Your breathing becomes a tangible reminder of the Holy Spirit's indwelling and an opportunity to surrender more fully to His guidance and power.

# The Synthesis: Breath as Divine Connection

Having explored the progressive revelation of divine breath through Ruach, Neshama, and Pneuma, you can now synthesize these concepts into a comprehensive understanding of breath as a sacred connection in your life. This synthesis operates on multiple levels:

1. **Theological Synthesis:** The three terms reveal a progressive revelation of God's breath in your spiritual journey—from the general concept of **divine breath/spirit (Ruach)** to the specialized divine breath

given to you as a human **(Neshama)** to the indwelling presence of the Holy Spirit in you as a believer **(Pneuma)**.

2. **Functional Synthesis**: Your breath is a practical means of engaging in spiritual realities. By consciously attending to your breath, you can become more aware of the Spirit's presence and more receptive to His guidance in your daily life.

3. **Experiential Synthesis**: The rhythm of your breathing parallels spiritual realities. Your inhalation represents receiving from God; your exhalation represents releasing to God. This pattern of receiving, releasing, taking in, and letting go mirrors the fundamental dynamic of your spiritual life.

4. **Transformational Synthesis:** Breath awareness can facilitate spiritual transformation. As you synchronize your breathing with scriptural truth and spiritual intentions, you align your whole being—body, soul, and spirit—with God's purposes for your life.

5. **Letter-Based Synthesis**: The Hebrew letters of Ruach and Neshama reveal that your breath carries God's holiness, connects Heaven and Earth, binds you to God, initiates faith, brings wholeness and peace, carries divine knowledge and lovingkindness, and reveals God's presence and light in your life.

## CHAPTER SIX:
### The Divine Mystery
### Of God's Breath of Life

The apostle Paul recognized this synthesis when he described Scripture as **"God-breathed"** (theopneustos) in **2 Timothy 3:16**. This term suggests that God's Word carries His breath or Spirit, making it living and active in your life rather than merely informational.

It's remarkable to consider that all this time, God's power has been right under your nose—literally—and you may not have been fully aware of it. The breath that flows through your nostrils moment by moment carries divine holiness, connects you to Heaven while grounding you on Earth, binds you to God, initiates faith, brings wholeness and peace, carries divine knowledge and lovingkindness, and reveals God's presence and light in your life.

# Biblical Passages on the Breath of God

Scripture reveals God's breath as powerful, creative, and transformative, directly impacting your spiritual life. Here are some key passages that illuminate this concept for your meditation practice:

**Job 33:4 -** "**The Spirit of God has made me, and the breath of the Almighty gives me life." (ESV)** This verse reaffirms the creation account, acknowledging that your existence depends on God's breath. It reminds you that your life is not self-generated but received as a gift from your Creator with each breath you take.

**Psalm 33:6 - "By the word of the LORD the heavens were made and by the breath of his mouth all their host." (ESV)** God's breath creatively and generatively brought the celestial bodies into existence. This reveals the power inherent in the divine breath you receive—it doesn't merely animate your existing being, but brings new realities into your life.

**Isaiah 11:4- "...and with the breath of his lips he shall kill the wicked."** This messianic prophecy depicts God's breath as an instrument of judgment, powerful enough to overthrow evil. It reminds us that the divine breath flowing through us is not neutral but aligned with God's righteousness and justice, empowering us to overcome sin.

**Ezekiel 37:5-6 "Thus says the Lord GOD to these bones: Behold, I will cause breath to enter you, and you shall live. And I will lay sinews upon you, cause flesh to come upon you, cover you with skin, and put breath in you, and you shall live, and you shall know that I am the LORD." (ESV)** In Ezekiel's vision of the valley of dry bones, God's breath resurrects the dead, restoring not just biological life but spiritual vitality. This passage reveals breath as the agent of revival and renewal in your spiritual journey, capable of bringing life to your dry and barren places.

**2 Timothy 3:16-17 "All Scripture is God-breathed and is profitable for teaching, for reproof, for correction, and for training in righteousness, that the man of God may be complete, equipped for every good work" (ESV).** Here, divine breath is associated with Scripture itself. God's Word carries His breath, making it living and active in your life rather than merely informational. When you engage with Scripture in meditation, you're engaging with God's breath.

**Revelation 11:11 - "Now after the three and a half days the breath of life from God entered them, and they stood up on their feet, and great fear fell on those who saw them." (NKJV)** God's breath resurrects the two witnesses in this apocalyptic vision, demonstrating divine power over death. This reinforces the connection between breath and resurrection life that you can experience even now as you practice breath-centered meditation.

These passages collectively reveal that God's breath is not merely a biological necessity in your life but a spiritual force that creates, animates, judges, resurrects, inspires, and transforms. When you consciously engage with your breath in meditation, you connect with this divine reality that permeates Scripture from Genesis to Revelation and continues to work in your life today.

# Practical Application: Breath-Centered Biblical Meditation

The progressive revelation of divine breath through Ruach, Neshama, and Pneuma, along with the profound insights from their Hebrew letters, transforms your approach to meditation. Rather than seeing controlled breathing as a relaxation technique, you can recognize it to engage more fully with the Holy Spirit who dwells within you.

Here are some practical approaches to breath-centered biblical meditation that integrate these concepts into your spiritual practice:

1. **Ruach Awareness Meditation**: Begin meditation by observing your breath for a few minutes. Notice the rhythm, depth, and quality of your breathing without trying to change it. As you observe, remember that your breath carries God's holiness, connects Heaven and Earth, and binds you to God. Whisper to yourself: "My breath carries God's holiness to me."

2. **Neshama Connection Practice**: As you breathe, consciously acknowledge that your breath initiates **faith, brings wholeness and peace, carries divine knowledge and lovingkindness, and reveals God's presence and light in your life.** With each inhalation, visualize receiving these divine qualities; release anything that hinders them with each exhalation. Say to yourself: "With each breath, I receive God's wholeness and peace."

3. **Pneuma Indwelling Meditation**: Focus on the reality that the Holy Spirit (Pneuma) dwells within you as a believer. As you breathe, affirm that your body is the temple of the Holy Spirit. Invite the Spirit to fill you more completely with each breath, surrendering more fully to His guidance and power. Pray: "Holy Spirit, fill me more completely with each breath I take."

CHAPTER SIX:
The Divine Mystery
Of God's Breath of Life

4. **Scripture Breathing:** Coordinate your breathing with Scripture verses that speak of God's breath or spirit. For example, breathe in while mentally reciting "The Spirit of God has made me" and breathe out while completing the verse, "and the breath of the Almighty gives me life" (Job 33:4). This practice integrates God's Word with the physical reminder of His sustaining presence in your life.

5. **Name-of-God Breathing**: Synchronize your breathing with the names or attributes of God that are meaningful to you. For instance, breathe in while mentally saying "Yahweh" (the covenant name of God) and breathe out while saying "Shalom" (peace). This practice aligns your physical rhythm with spiritual truth and deepens your awareness of God's character.

6. **Breath Prayers:** Develop short, one-sentence prayers synchronizing with breathing. You can divide the ancient "Jesus Prayer" ("Lord Jesus Christ, Son of God, have mercy on me, a sinner") between inhalation and exhalation. You can use these breath prayers throughout your day to maintain spiritual awareness, even when busy.

7. **Hebrew Letter Meditation**: Meditate on the meanings of the Hebrew letters in Ruach and Neshama that you've discovered. As you inhale, focus on receiving God's holiness (**Resh**), connection to Heaven (**Vav**), binding with God (**Cheth**), emergence of faith (**Nun**),

wholeness and peace (**Shin**), divine knowledge and lovingkindness (**Mem**), and God's presence and light (**Heh**). As you exhale, visualize these qualities flowing through your entire being. Affirm: "These divine qualities are becoming part of who I am."

8. **Isaiah 11:2 Ruach Meditation**: As you breathe, focus on each of the six manifestations of the Spirit mentioned in Isaiah 11:2. With each inhalation, mentally receive one aspect of the **Ruach: wisdom, understanding, counsel, might, knowledge, or fear of the Lord**. With each exhalation, imagine that quality flowing through your being and empowering your life. This practice helps you consciously engage with the supernatural benefits of the Ruach.

These practices are not ends but means of engaging more fully with the Holy Spirit within you. We aim not for mere controlled breathing, but for deeper communion with the God who breathes life into you moment by moment.

# Conclusion: The Integrated Divine Breath

As you conclude your exploration of the divine breath through Ruach, Neshama, and Pneuma—and the profound revelations in their Hebrew letters—recognize that your physical breathing is a continuous reminder of your dependence on God and your connection to His Spirit. Every breath you take can serve as a moment of communion with the Creator who breathed life into Adam, continues to sustain you through His Spirit, and dwells within you through Christ.

The progressive revelation of divine breath in Scripture—from the general concept of Ruach to the specialized divine breath of Neshama, to the indwelling presence of the Holy Spirit as Pneuma — provides a comprehensive theological foundation for your Christian meditation practice. This foundation transforms your breathing from a mere biological function into a sacred practice that connects you with the very life of God.

It reveals that the Breath of Life you receive from God also provides His spiritual, supernatural power. His Breath of life flows and fills you with the power to strengthen your ability to rule over stress, anxiety, depression, anger, rage, addictions, footholds, and whatever else your sinful nature tries to strangle you with.

As you move forward in your meditation journey, remember that breathing is not merely a biological function but a sacred connection to the God who gives you life. Each breath is an opportunity to acknowledge your dependence, express your gratitude, and surrender more fully to the Spirit's work within you.

# CHAPTER SIX:
## The Divine Mystery
## Of God's Breath of Life

May your breathing constantly remind you of the divine breath that animates your being and connects you to the eternal God who sustains all life. It's remarkable to think that all this time, God's very power has been under your nose, and now you have the awareness to embrace it fully.

# CHAPTER SEVEN:
# Christian Breathwork Foundations

Various spiritual traditions have recognized the profound connection between breath and spiritual experience throughout history. Scripture, beginning with God breathing life into Adam and continuing with the Holy Spirit's indwelling in believers, grounds this connection in the Christian tradition. This chapter will explore the biblical foundations for Christian breathwork, develop practical techniques aligned with Scripture, and enhance meditation practice.

## The Biblical Basis for Breathwork

As we've already discovered, the biblical words for "spirit"— Ruach in Hebrew and Pneuma in Greek—also mean "breath" or "wind." This linguistic connection reveals a profound spiritual truth: our spiritual life is intimately connected to our breathing. Let's examine several key biblical passages that establish this connection:

**Genesis 2:7 - "Then the LORD God formed man of dust from the ground and breathed into his nostrils the breath of life, and man became a living being." (NIV)** This foundational text establishes breath as God's life-giving gift.

The Hebrew phrase **"Nishmat Chayyim"** (נִשְׁמַת חַיִּים) (breath of life) shows that breath carries the essence of life itself, not merely biological animation, but spiritual vitality.

**Job 33:4 - "The Spirit of God has made me, and the breath of the Almighty gives me life." (ESV)** Job acknowledges that his very existence depends on God's breath. This verse reminds us that breathing is not merely an autonomous biological function, but a continuous gift from our Creator.

**Psalm 150:6 - "Let everything that has breath praise the LORD. Praise the LORD!" (ESV)** This last verse of the Psalter connects breath with worship, suggesting that every breath can be an act of praise to the One who gives it.

**Ezekiel 37:5-6 - "Thus says the Lord GOD to these bones: Behold, I will cause breath to enter you, and you shall live. And I will lay sinews upon you, and will cause flesh to come upon you, and cover you with skin, and put breath in you, and you shall live, and you shall know that I am the LORD."(ESV)** In Ezekiel's vision of the valley of dry bones, God's breath brings the dead back to life, restoring biological life and spiritual vitality to Israel. This passage reveals breath as the agent of revival and renewal.

**John 20:22 - "And when He had said this, He breathed on them and said to them, Receive the Holy Spirit." (ESV)** Jesus deliberately echoes the creation account, breathing on His disciples to symbolize the Holy Spirit's impartation. This action establishes a direct connection between physical breath and spiritual empowerment.

[91]

**Acts 17:25 - "...nor is He served by human hands, as though He needed anything since He Himself gives to all mankind life and breath and everything." (ESV)** Paul reminds the Athenians that God is the source of all breath, emphasizing our moment-by-moment dependence on divine sustenance.

These passages collectively establish a biblical foundation for Christian breathwork. They reveal that breath is a divine gift that sustains life, a continuous reminder of our dependence on God, a means of spiritual renewal and revival, a vehicle for the Holy Spirit's presence and power, and **a natural expression of worship and praise.**

This biblical understanding distinguishes Christian breathwork from practices rooted in other spiritual traditions. While the techniques may sometimes appear similar, the theological frameworks and spiritual intentions differ.

# Distinguishing Christian
## Breathwork from Eastern Practices

Many Christians hesitate to engage with breathwork because it is associated with Eastern spiritual practices such as pranayama in yoga or various Buddhist breathing techniques. This hesitation is understandable, as these practices often emerge from worldviews that conflict with biblical Christianity. However, it's important to distinguish between the method itself and the theological framework in which it's practiced.

Breath control is not inherently Eastern or non-Christian. It's a universal human capacity that God designed for our physiology. Just as prayer, though practiced across religions, takes on distinct meaning within Christianity, so too can breathwork be practiced within a biblical framework that honors Christ and aligns with Scripture.

Here are key distinctions between Christian breathwork and Eastern approaches:

1. **Source of Life**: In Christian breathwork, we recognize breath as God's gift, sustaining us through His grace. Eastern traditions often view breath (prana, chi, etc.) as an impersonal cosmic energy to harness for spiritual advancement.

2. **Spiritual Goal:** Christian breathwork aims to enhance our communion with the personal God revealed in Scripture and to align our being with His purposes. Eastern practices typically seek states of consciousness that transcend personal identity or union with an impersonal absolute.

3. **Christian breathwork draws its foundation from the biblical understanding of creation, fall, redemption, and restoration.** It acknowledges human sinfulness, the necessity of Christ's atonement, and the Holy Spirit's indwelling presence. Eastern approaches operate from different assumptions about reality, humanity, and spiritual development.

4. **Relational Focus**: Christian breathwork facilitates a relationship with God through Christ, enhancing our awareness of the Holy Spirit's presence and guidance.

Eastern practices often aim at self-realization or enlightenment without reference to a personal Creator.

5. **Christian breathwork:** uses breath to engage with revealed truth, which is informed by and aligned with biblical teaching. Eastern approaches typically draw from different textual traditions and philosophical systems.

These distinctions don't mean we must reject all breathing techniques associated with other traditions. Instead, we can discerningly adapt techniques that align with biblical principles while reframing them within a Christian theological framework. This approach follows Paul's principle of **"testing everything and holding fast to what is good" (1 Thessalonians 5:21).**

# Breath as Prayer and Connection

In the Christian tradition, breath has long been associated with prayer. The ancient practice of "breath prayer" involves synchronizing short prayers with the rhythm of breathing, creating a continuous communion with God throughout daily activities. This practice aligns perfectly with Paul's exhortation to **"pray without ceasing" (1 Thessalonians 5:17)**. The connection between breath and prayer appears in various Christian traditions:

- The Eastern Orthodox tradition developed the "Jesus Prayer" ("Lord Jesus Christ, Son of God, have mercy on me, a sinner"), which is often synchronized with breathing—inhaling during the first half and exhaling during the second half.

- The Western contemplative tradition includes practices like "centering prayer," which use breath awareness to facilitate inner silence and receptivity to God's presence.

- The monastic tradition incorporated rhythmic breathing into the practice of Lectio Divina (sacred reading), using breath to punctuate the movement between reading, meditation, prayer, and contemplation.

These historical practices recognize that breath is a natural bridge between body and spirit, helping to integrate our physical and spiritual dimensions in prayer. By consciously connecting our breathing with worship, we transform an automatic bodily function into a means of continuous communion with God.

This approach aligns with **Romans 12:1**, which calls us to present our bodies as **"living sacrifices, holy and acceptable to God."** We embody this scriptural principle when we offer our breathing, one of our most fundamental bodily functions, as a vehicle for prayer and communion.

Breath prayer also helps fulfill Jesus's teaching about the greatest commandment**: "You shall love the Lord your God with all your heart and with all your soul and with all your mind and with all your strength." Mark 12:30 (ESV)**. By engaging our physical breathing (strength) in prayer, we unite it with our emotions (heart), will (soul), and thoughts (mind) in loving God.

# Practical Breathwork Techniques for Christians

Now, explore specific breathwork techniques that align with biblical principles and enhance Christian meditation. These practices deepen your awareness of God's presence, facilitate engagement with Scripture, and strengthen your spiritual life.

## 1. Breath Awareness Practice

This foundational practice involves noticing your breath without attempting to control it. It serves as an entry point to meditative consciousness and a reminder of God's sustaining presence.

**Technique:** - Find a comfortable, quiet place to sit with your spine relatively straight. - Close your eyes or lower your gaze. Place one hand on your chest and one on your abdomen to feel the movement of your breath. - Observe your natural breathing pattern for 3-5 minutes. - When your mind wanders (which is normal), gently return your attention to your breath. As you observe your breathing, remember that each breath is God's gift—the same divine breath that animated Adam and continues to sustain your life.

**Scripture Connection: "For in him we live and move and have our being." Acts 17:28 (NIV)**

**Spiritual Benefit**: This practice cultivates awareness of your dependence on God and helps establish the present-moment attention needed to hear God's voice.

## 2. Scripture Breathing

This practice coordinates your breathing with Scripture, helping you internalize God's Word and integrate it into your physical being.

**Technique**: - Select a short Scripture verse or phrase that resonates with you. - Divide it into two parts—one for inhalation and one for exhalation. - Breathe in slowly while mentally reciting the first part. - Breathe out slowly while mentally reciting the second part. - Continue this rhythm for 5-10 minutes, allowing the Scripture to sink deeply into your consciousness.

**Examples**: - Inhale: **"The Lord is my shepherd."** Exhale: **"I shall not want"** (Psalm 23:1) - Inhale: **"Be still."** Exhale: **"And know that I am God"** (Psalm 46:10) - Inhale: **"Create in me a clean heart, O God."** Exhale: **"And renew a right spirit within me"** (Psalm 51:10)

**Scripture Connection**: **"Let the word of Christ dwell in you richly in all wisdom, teaching and admonishing one another in psalms and hymns and spiritual songs, singing with grace in your hearts to the Lord." Colossians 3:16.**

**Spiritual Benefit**: This practice helps Scripture move from intellectual understanding to embodied knowledge, integrating God's Word into your breathing.

## 3. Trinitarian Breath Prayer

This practice honors the Trinity through a three-part breathing pattern, acknowledging each person of the Godhead.

**Technique**: - Sit comfortably with your spine straight, eyes closed, or gaze lowered. - Inhale slowly, mentally addressing God the Father: **"Heavenly Father..."** Hold the breath briefly, mentally addressing God the Son: **"Lord Jesus Christ..."** - Exhale slowly, mentally addressing God the Spirit: **"Holy Spirit..."** - Continue this pattern for 5-10 minutes, allowing your breathing to become a Trinitarian prayer.

**Scripture Connection: "The grace of the Lord Jesus Christ and the love of God and the fellowship of the Holy Spirit be with you all." 2 Corinthians 13:14 (ESV)**

**Spiritual Benefit**: This practice deepens your relationship with each person of the Trinity and embodies the theological truth that we live and move within the life of the triune God.

## 4. Breath of Surrender

This practice uses breathing to facilitate surrender to God's will, releasing control and receiving grace.

**Technique**: - Sit or lie in a comfortable position. - As you inhale, mentally name something you need to receive from God (peace, wisdom, strength, etc.). - As you exhale, mentally name something you need to release to God (fear, control, pride, etc.). - Continue this pattern for 5-10 minutes, allowing each breath to become an exchange of surrender and reception.

**Examples**: - Inhale: **"Your peace"** Exhale: **"My anxiety"** - Inhale: **"Your wisdom"** Exhale: **"My confusion"** - Inhale: **"Your strength"** Exhale: **"My weakness."**

**Scripture Connection**: "Cast all your anxiety on him because he cares for you" (1 Peter 5:7).

**Spiritual Benefit**: This practice embodies the spiritual rhythm of dying to self and living to Christ, helping you release what hinders your spiritual growth and receive what nurtures it.

## 5. Intercessory Breath Prayer

This practice uses breathing to intercede for others, embodying the biblical call to **"pray for one another"** **(James 5:16).**

**Technique**: Begin with breath awareness for a few minutes. –Bring someone who needs prayer to mind. - As you inhale, mentally receive God's love and compassion for this person. - As you exhale, mentally direct that love and compassion toward them. - Continue for several breaths, then move to another person. - Conclude by thanking God for His work in each person's life.

**Scripture Connection: "And pray in the Spirit on all occasions with all kinds of prayers and requests. With this in mind, be alert and always keep praying for all the Lord's people." Ephesians 6:18. (NIV)**

**Spiritual Benefit**: This practice helps you embody Christ's compassion for others and take part in the Holy Spirit's intercessory work.

# Overcoming Anxiety and Stress Through Sacred Breathing

One of the most immediate benefits of Christian breathwork is its effectiveness in addressing anxiety and stress, common challenges in our fast-paced, pressure-filled world. Scripture acknowledges these struggles: **"Do not be anxious about anything" (Philippians 4:6) and "Cast all your anxiety on him because he cares for you" (1 Peter 5:7).**

Anxiety often manifests physically through rapid, shallow breathing, which triggers the body's stress response. By consciously slowing and deepening the breath, we can activate the parasympathetic nervous system (the "rest and digest" response), calming both body and mind. The following sacred breathing technique explicitly addresses anxiety and stress from a Christian perspective:

## Peace Breathing Practice

**To begin, find a quiet place to avoid disturbances.** –Sit comfortably with your spine straight but not rigid. - Place one hand on your chest and one on your abdomen. - Take a slow, deep breath through your nose, allowing your abdomen to expand (rather than your chest). - Hold your breath briefly. - Exhale slowly through your mouth, extending the exhalation longer than the inhalation.

As you breathe, mentally recite: **"The peace of Christ, which transcends all understanding, guards my heart and mind" (based on Philippians 4:7**). - Continue for 5-10 minutes, allowing your body to relax and your mind to be filled with God's peace.

**Scripture Connection**: **"Peace I leave with you; my peace, I give you. I do not give to you as the world gives. Do not let your hearts be troubled and do not be afraid." John 14:27(NIV)**

**Spiritual Benefit**: This practice embodies receiving Christ's peace, which He specifically distinguished from the world's temporary relief. It helps transform anxiety into an opportunity for deeper trust and reliance on God.

When practiced regularly, this technique can become a powerful tool for managing anxiety at the moment. Rather than being controlled by anxious thoughts and feelings, you can use sacred breathing to return to meditative consciousness and remember God's presence and promises.

# Integrating Breathwork into Your Daily Spiritual Rhythm

To experience the full benefits of Christian breathwork, it's essential to integrate these practices into your daily spiritual rhythm. Here are suggestions for incorporating breathwork throughout your day:

1. **Morning Awakening**: Begin each day with 5 minutes of breath awareness, acknowledging God's gift of life

and inviting the Holy Spirit's guidance for the day ahead.

2. **Scripture Meditation**: Incorporate Scripture breathing into your daily Bible reading, allowing God's Word to be integrated with your breath.

3. **Transition Moments**: Use brief breath prayers during transitions between activities—before meetings, when entering or leaving your home, while waiting in line, etc.

4. **Stress Response**: When you notice anxiety or stress arising, pause for 30 seconds and breathe, remembering Christ's promise of peace.

5. **Evening Review**: End your day with the breath of surrender, releasing the day's events to God and receiving His perspective and peace.

These integrations don't require additional time in your schedule, but transform ordinary moments into opportunities for spiritual connection. They help fulfill Paul's exhortation to **"pray without ceasing" (1 Thessalonians 5:17)** by weaving prayer into the fabric of daily life through the medium of breath.

# Conclusion: Breathing as Spiritual Practice

As we conclude our exploration of Christian breathwork, remember that these practices are not ends but means of deepening your relationship with God through Christ. The goal is not a perfect technique but growing awareness of and responsiveness to the Holy Spirit who dwells within you.

Breathwork serves as a tangible reminder of profound spiritual truths: your moment-by-moment dependence on God, the Holy Spirit's indwelling presence, and your participation in the divine life through Christ. You transform an automatic physical function into a sacred connection with your Creator by consciously engaging in your breath.

In the next chapter, we'll explore the role of the Holy Spirit as a guide in your meditation practice, and discover how to discern His voice and follow His leading on your spiritual journey. The breathwork techniques you've learned will serve as a foundation for this more profound exploration of Spirit-led meditation.

As you incorporate these practices into your life, may each breath become a reminder of God's sustaining presence and an opportunity for deeper communion with the One who breathed life into you and continues to sustain you moment by moment.

## CHAPTER EIGHT:
# The Holy Spirit as Guide

In our journey through biblical meditation, we've explored the linguistic foundations in Hebrew and Greek, examined the scientific evidence for meditation's benefits, discovered the profound connection between breath and spirit, and learned practical breathwork techniques. Now, we turn to perhaps the most essential aspect of Christian meditation: the guidance of the Holy Spirit.

## Understanding the Trinity

To fully appreciate the Holy Spirit's role in meditation, we must first understand His place within the Trinity. The doctrine of the Trinity—that God exists eternally as three persons in one essence—is foundational to the Christian faith, though it transcends complete human comprehension.

The Trinity is not a hierarchy but a perfect communion of three co-equal, co-eternal persons: the Father, Son, and Holy Spirit. Each person is fully God, yet there is only one God. This mystery reflects the relational nature of God's being—He exists in a perfect relationship within Himself.

Scripture reveals this Trinitarian nature in various passages:

- At Jesus's baptism, the Spirit descends like a dove as the Father speaks from heaven (**Matthew 3:16-17**).

- Jesus commands baptism **"in the name of the Father and the Son and of the Holy Spirit" (Matthew 28:19).**

- Paul's benediction invokes **"the grace of the Lord Jesus Christ and the love of God and the fellowship of the Holy Spirit" (2 Corinthians 13:14**).

- Peter addresses believers as **"elect according to the foreknowledge of God the Father, in sanctification of the Spirit, for obedience and sprinkling of the blood of Jesus Christ," 1 Peter 1:2. (NKJV)**

These passages reveal that each person of the Trinity plays a distinct yet harmonious role in our salvation and spiritual formation. The Father starts, the Son accomplishes, and the Spirit applies. This Trinitarian framework is essential for understanding the Holy Spirit's guidance in meditation.

When we engage in Christian meditation, we're not seeking an impersonal cosmic force or our own higher consciousness. We're entering communion with the triune God—approaching the Father through the Son, by the power of the Holy Spirit. This Trinitarian understanding distinguishes Christian meditation from other forms of spiritual practice.

# The Person and Work of the Holy Spirit

The Holy Spirit is not an impersonal force or energy, but the third person of the Trinity—fully divine and engaged with believers. Scripture reveals many personal attributes of the Spirit:

- He speaks (Acts 13:2)
- He intercedes (Romans 8:26-27)
- He teaches (John 14:26)
- He can be grieved (Ephesians 4:30)
- He distributes gifts as He wills (1 Corinthians 12:11)

These attributes reveal that our relationship with the Holy Spirit is personal and relational, not mechanical or manipulative. We don't control the Spirit through techniques or formulas; we commune with Him as a divine person who indwells us.

The Holy Spirit's work encompasses various aspects of the Christian life:

1. **Regeneration**: The Spirit gives new spiritual life to believers (John 3:5-8).
2. **Indwelling**: The Spirit permanently lives within believers (1 Corinthians 6:19).
3. **Sealing**: The Spirit marks believers as God's possession (Ephesians 1:13-14).
4. **Filling:** The Spirit empowers believers for service and witness (Acts 4:31).
5. **Sanctification**: The Spirit transforms believers into Christ's likeness (2 Corinthians 3:18).
6. **Illumination**: The Spirit helps believers understand Scripture (1 Corinthians 2:12-14).

7. **Guidance**: The Spirit directs believers in God's will (Romans 8:14).

8. **Gifting**: The Spirit equips believers for ministry (1 Corinthians 12:4-11).

9. **Intercession**: The Spirit prays through believers according to God's will (Romans 8:26-27).

10. **Fruit-bearing**: The Spirit produces a Christlike character in believers (Galatians 5:22-23).

The Holy Spirit's roles as indweller, illuminator, guide, and intercessor are significant in meditation. He transforms meditation from a human-centered activity into a divine-human communion in which God actively participates.

# Historical Manifestations of the Holy Spirit

Throughout biblical and church history, the Holy Spirit has manifested His presence and power in various ways. Understanding these historical manifestations helps us recognize and respond to the Spirit's work in our meditation practice.

In the Old Testament, the Spirit typically came upon specific individuals temporarily for particular tasks.

- He empowered leaders like Moses and the seventy elders (Numbers 11:16-17, 25).

- He equipped craftsmen like Bezalel for tabernacle construction (Exodus 31:3).

- He enabled judges like Samson for military victories (Judges 14:6).
- He inspired prophets like Isaiah to speak God's word (Isaiah 61:1).

These temporary empowerments pointed to an incredible greater promise—that God would one day pour out His Spirit on all His people. The prophet Joel proclaimed: **"And it shall come to pass afterward, that I will pour out my Spirit on all flesh; your sons and your daughters shall prophesy, your old men shall dream dreams, and your young men shall see visions. Even on the male and female servants in those days, I will pour out my Spirit." Joel 2:28-29 (ESV)**

This promise found initial fulfillment at Pentecost, when the Holy Spirit descended on the gathered disciples with visible and audible manifestations — **"a sound like a mighty rushing wind" and "divided tongues as of fire" (Acts 2:2-3)**. This dramatic event marked a new era in the Spirit's work, characterized by His permanent indwelling of all believers.

Throughout church history, the Spirit has continued to manifest in various ways:

- In the early church, He empowered believers to be bold witnesses despite persecution (Acts 4:31).
- During the monastic movement, He led believers into contemplative communion with God through silence and solitude.
- In revival movements, He brought conviction of sin and spiritual awakening to entire communities.

[108]

- In the charismatic renewal, He restored awareness of spiritual gifts and supernatural manifestations.
- In the global expansion of Christianity, He has empowered cross-cultural witness and indigenous expressions of faith.

These historical manifestations remind us that the Holy Spirit does not limit Himself to one mode of operation or expression. He works in diverse ways across cultures, traditions, and historical periods, always pointing to Christ and advancing God's kingdom.

In our meditation practice, we should remain open to the Spirit's diverse manifestations while testing everything against Scripture (1 Thessalonians 5:19-21). The Spirit may guide us through subtle impressions, Scripture illumination, prophetic insights, or other means, but His guidance will always align with His revealed Word.

# Symbols and Representations in Scripture

Scripture uses symbols to represent the Holy Spirit, each revealing aspects of His nature and work. Understanding these symbols enriches our awareness of how the Spirit might manifest in our meditation practice.

## Dove

At Jesus's baptism, **"the Holy Spirit descended on him in bodily form, like a dove" (Luke 3:22).** The dove symbolizes:

- **Purity**: In the sacrificial system, those who couldn't afford lambs offered doves, representing accessible purity.
- **Peace**: In Noah's story, the dove returned with an olive branch, signaling the end of judgment and the dawn of a new creation.
- **Gentleness**: The dove's nature reflects the Spirit's gentle, non-coercive guidance rather than forceful control.

In meditation, the Spirit often works with dove-like gentleness, not overwhelming our consciousness but gently guiding our thoughts and impressions toward truth.

## Fire

At Pentecost, **"divided tongues as of fire appeared to them and rested on each one of them" (Acts 2:3)**. Fire symbolizes:

- **Purification**: Fire refines precious metals by burning away impurities, just as the Spirit purifies our hearts.
- **Passion**: Fire generates heat and energy, reflecting the Spirit's role in kindling holy passion and zeal.
- **Transformation**: Fire changes whatever it touches, just as the Spirit transforms us into Christ's image.

In meditation, we may experience the Spirit's fire as a conviction of sin, purification of motives, or ignition of holy desire for God and His purposes.

## Wind

Jesus compared the Spirit to the wind: "The wind blows where it wishes, and you hear its sound, but you do not know where it comes from or where it goes. So, it is with everyone who is born of the Spirit" (John 3:8). Wind symbolizes:

- **Invisibility yet Power**: Like the wind, the Spirit is invisible, but His effects are evident.
- **Sovereignty:** Nothing controls or predicts wind, reflecting the Spirit's sovereign freedom.
- **Movement**: Wind creates movement, just as the Spirit brings dynamism and progress to our spiritual life.

In meditation, the Spirit's wind-like quality reminds us we cannot manipulate or control His guidance—we can only create conditions that welcome His sovereign movement.

## Water

Jesus declares, "**Whoever believes in me, as the Scripture has said, out of his heart will flow rivers of living water.**" John explains, "**Now this he spoke concerning the Spirit.**" **John 7:38-39. (NKJV)**

Water symbolizes:

- **Cleansing:** Water washes away impurity as the Spirit cleanses us from sin.
- **Life-giving**: Water sustains life, as the Spirit imparts spiritual vitality.

[111]

- **Satisfaction**: Water quenches thirst, as the Spirit satisfies our deepest longings.

In meditation, the Spirit's water-like quality may manifest as inner refreshment, cleansing of conscience, or satisfying spiritual thirst.

## Oil

In the Old Testament, anointing with oil symbolized the Spirit's empowerment, as seen in David's anointing: "**Then Samuel took the horn of oil and anointed him in the midst of his brothers. And the Spirit of the LORD rushed upon David from that day forward. And Samuel rose up and went to Ramah.**" 1 Samuel 16:13 (ESV) Oil symbolizes:

- **Consecration**: Oil sets apart people or objects for sacred use, as the Spirit sets us apart for God.
- **Healing:** Medicinal use of oil reflected the Spirit's healing work in our brokenness.
- **Empowerment**: Oil-enabled lamps to burn, symbolizing the Spirit's empowerment for service.

In meditation, the Spirit's oil-like quality may manifest as a sense of consecration for specific, inner healing of emotional wounds or empowerment for particular callings.

These biblical symbols provide a framework for recognizing the Spirit's diverse manifestations in our meditation experience. Rather than expecting one manifestation, we should remain open to how the Spirit might guide, comfort, convict, or empower us as we meditate.

# Building a Relationship with the Holy Spirit

The Holy Spirit is not merely a power to be accessed or a resource to be used, but a divine person with whom we're called to build a relationship. This relational dimension distinguishes Christian meditation from technique-focused approaches.

Here are practical steps for building a relationship with the Holy Spirit in your meditation practice:

## 1. Acknowledge His Presence

Begin your meditation by consciously acknowledging the Holy Spirit's presence within you. This isn't about generating feelings, but recognizing the biblical truth that if you're a believer, the Spirit dwells in you (1 Corinthians 6:19). A simple prayer like "Holy Spirit, I acknowledge Your presence within me" establishes the relational foundation for your meditation.

## 2. Invite His Guidance

While the Spirit already indwells believers, we still benefit from inviting His guidance in our meditation. Jesus taught, **"How much more will the heavenly Father give the Holy Spirit to those who ask him!" (Luke 11:13)**. This invitation expresses your dependence on divine guidance rather than self-directed efforts.

## 3. Listen Expectantly

A relationship involves two-way communication. After speaking to the Spirit through prayer, create space to listen for His response. This listening isn't passive but expectant—anticipating that the Spirit will guide your thoughts, bring Scripture to mind, or impress truth upon your heart. As Jesus says, **"My sheep hear my voice" (John 10:27).**

## 4. Respond Obediently

Relationship with the Spirit grows through responsive obedience. When you sense His guidance during meditation—whether to confess sin, extend forgiveness, take a specific action, or rest in God's love—respond with willing obedience. Jesus taught obedience deepens the relationship: **"Whoever has my commandments and keeps them, he it is who loves me...and I will love him and manifest myself to him." John 14:21 (ESV).**

## 5. Express Gratitude

Acknowledge the Spirit's work in your meditation with specific gratitude. Thank Him for insights gained, comfort received, conviction experienced, or simply for His faithful presence. Gratitude cultivates awareness of the Spirit's ongoing activity and prevents taking His guidance for granted.

## 6. Practice Continual Communion

Extend your relationship with the Spirit beyond designated meditation times into everyday life. Paul exhorts believers to

**"pray without ceasing" (1 Thessalonians 5:17**) and to **"be filled with the Spirit" (Ephesians 5:18**)—a continuous process rather than a one-time event. The breathwork techniques explored in the previous chapter can facilitate this continual communion.

## 7. Learn His Voice

Like any relationship, knowing the Spirit's voice comes through regular interaction and familiarity with His character, as revealed in Scripture. Jesus says, **"When the Spirit of truth comes, he will guide you into all the truth." John 16:13 (ESV)** The Spirit's guidance will always align with biblical truth, Christ's character, and the Spirit's fruit (Galatians 5:22-23).

## 8. Honor His Personhood

Avoid treating the Holy Spirit as an impersonal force or tool for spiritual advancement. Honor His personhood by directly addressing Him, respecting His sovereign timing, and recognizing that you cannot reduce the relationship to techniques or formulas. The Spirit **"apportions to each one individually as he wills" (1 Corinthians 12:11**), not as we demand.

As you implement these practices, your meditation will transform from a self-directed exercise into a divine-human encounter. The Holy Spirit becomes not just the object of theological understanding, but the active guide and companion in your spiritual journey.

# Discerning the Spirit's Voice in Meditation

One of the most common questions about Spirit-led meditation is: "How do I know if what I'm hearing is the Holy Spirit or just my thoughts?" This question reflects a legitimate concern for discernment, which Scripture encourages: **"Beloved, do not believe every spirit, but test the spirits to see whether they are from God." 1 John 4:1 (ESV)**

While discernment is a lifelong learning process, Scripture provides several criteria for recognizing the Spirit's guidance:

## 1. Alignment with Scripture

The Spirit who inspired Scripture (2 Peter 1:21) will never contradict it. Any guidance that conflicts with the clear teaching of God's Word comes from another source. As you meditate, compare impressions or insights with biblical teaching, recognizing that the Spirit often speaks through bringing Scripture to mind.

## 2. Exaltation of Christ

**Jesus says the Spirit "will glorify me, for he will take what is mine and declare it to you" (John 16:14).** The Spirit consistently points to Christ rather than drawing attention to Himself or elevating human beings. Guidance that diminishes Jesus or elevates others above Him is not from the Holy Spirit.

## 3. Fruit of the Spirit

Guidance from the Holy Spirit will produce the fruit described in **Galatians 5:22-23: "love, joy, peace, patience, kindness, goodness, faithfulness, gentleness, self-control."** If an impression leads to anxiety, harshness, impulsivity, or other qualities contrary to this fruit, it likely comes from another source.

## 4. Community Confirmation

The Spirit typically works through the body of Christ, not just isolated individuals. Paul actually instructs others to **"weigh"** prophecies **(1 Corinthians 14:29)**. When you receive signif-icant guidance in meditation, seek confirmation from mature believers who know Scripture and demonstrate the fruit of the Spirit.

## 5. Inner Witness

**Romans 8:16 states, "The Spirit himself bears witness with our spirit that we are children of God." (ESV)** This inner witness—a deep sense of resonance and recognition—often accompanies the Spirit's authentic guidance. While subjective, this criterion complements the more objective standards above.

## 6. Humble Uncertainty

Paradoxically, the Spirit often leads with what theologian Parker Palmer calls "humble uncertainty"—confidence in the direction without dogmatic certainty about every detail. Both prideful certainty ("I know exactly what God is saying and anyone who disagrees is wrong") and fearful indecision ("I can never know what God is saying") often shows guidance from other sources.

## 7. Timing and Persistence

The Spirit's guidance often comes with divine timing—not too early (creating restless impatience) or too late (creating missed opportunities). Authentic guidance persists and deepens over time rather than appearing once and disappearing completely.

These criteria work together rather than in isolation. No single criterion is sufficient, but collectively, they provide a framework for discerning the Spirit's voice among the many voices that compete for our attention.

In practical terms, you might implement these criteria in your meditation through a simple process:

1. **Receive**: Be open to thoughts, impressions, or Scriptures that come to mind during meditation.
2. **Record**: Write down what you receive without immediate judgment.
3. **Review**: Examine what you've recorded against the criteria above.
4. **Respond**: Act on guidance that passes the discernment test; set aside guidance that doesn't.

This process honors the Spirit's desire to guide and the biblical call to discernment. Over time, you'll develop greater familiarity with the Spirit's voice, just as a sheep learns to recognize the shepherd's voice through repeated exposure (John 10:4-5).

# The Spirit's Guidance in Different Meditations

The Holy Spirit guides believers through various forms of meditation, each with distinct purposes and expressions. Understanding these different types helps us cooperate more fully with the Spirit's work in our spiritual formation.

## 1. Scripture Meditation

In Scripture meditation, the Holy Spirit fulfills Jesus's promise: **"But The Helper, the Holy Spirit, whom the Father will send in my name, he will teach you all things and bring to your remembrance all that I have said to you" John 14:26 (ESV)** The Spirit illuminates the meaning of Scripture, applies it to our specific circumstances, and brings relevant passages to the mind.

When meditating on Scripture, cooperate with the Spirit by prayerfully reading and asking for illumination, lingering on significant passages, noticing connections between different scriptures, and making a personal application of the text rather than an abstract, obedient response to what is revealed.

## 2. Contemplative Meditation

In contemplative meditation, which focuses on God's presence rather than analytical thinking, the Spirit fulfills Paul's prayer: **"that according to the riches of his glory, he**

**may grant you to be strengthened with power through his Spirit in your inner being, so that Christ may dwell in your hearts through faith." Ephesians 3:16-17 (ESV)**

The Spirit makes Christ's presence real to our consciousness. When practicing contemplative meditation, cooperate with the Spirit by simplifying your focus to God's presence, releasing distractions without frustration, resting in divine love rather than striving for experiences, remaining receptive to whatever the Spirit wishes to impart, and treasuring moments of communion without trying to manufacture them.

## 3. Creation Meditation

In creation meditation, which contemplates God through His works, the Spirit fulfills the psalmist's experience: "**When I look at your heavens, the work of your fingers, the moon and the stars, which you have set in place, what is man that you are mindful of him ₄ the son of man that you care for him?" Psalm 8:3-4 (ESV)**. The Spirit reveals the Creator through creation.

When meditating on creation, cooperate with the Spirit by:
**Observing:** natural details with wonder and attention
**Looking:** beyond the surface to spiritual significance
**Connecting**: creation's beauty with the Creator's character
**Allowing:** nature to prompt worship and gratitude, and
**Receiving:** creation as a book of divine revelation alongside Scripture.

## 4. Examen Meditation

In the meditation of examen, which prayerfully reviews daily life, the Spirit fulfills David's prayer: **"Search me, O God, and know my heart! Try me and know my thoughts! And see if there be any grievous way in me and lead me in the way everlasting!" Psalm 139:23-24 (ESV)** The Spirit reveals areas needing attention and affirms God's work.

When practicing examen, cooperate with the Spirit by reviewing your day without self-judgment or defensiveness, noticing patterns of thought, emotion, and behavior, discerning God's presence in ordinary moments, confessing failures with confidence in God's forgiveness, and expressing gratitude for divine guidance and provision.

## 5. Intercessory Meditation

In intercessory meditation, which focuses on praying for others, the Spirit fulfills Paul's teaching: **"Likewise, the Spirit helps us in our weakness. For we do not know what to pray for as we ought, but the Spirit himself intercedes for us with groanings too deep for words" Romans 8:26 (ESV).** The Spirit guides our prayers according to God's will.

When practicing intercessory meditation, cooperate with the Spirit by:

- **Beginning** with silence to discern prayer priorities.

- **Following** internal promptings about who needs prayer.

- **Remaining** open to unexpected directions in prayer.

- **Trusting** the Spirit's intercession beyond your words.

- **Believing** that Spirit-led prayer accomplishes God's purposes.

The Holy Spirit guides each type of meditation uniquely, according to its particular focus and purpose. By recognizing these distinct expressions of guidance, we can cooperate more fully with the Spirit's work in our spiritual formation.

# Conclusion: Yielding to the Spirit's Guidance

As we conclude our exploration of the Holy Spirit as a guide in meditation, remember that the ultimate purpose of His guidance is transformation into Christ's likeness. Paul writes, **"And we all, with unveiled face, beholding the glory of the Lord, are being transformed into the same image from one glory to another. For this comes from the Lord who is the Spirit." 2 Corinthians 3:18 (NIV)**

This transformation occurs not through human effort or technique, but through yielding to the Spirit's guidance moment by moment. As you continue your meditation journey, cultivate this posture of yielded receptivity—not passively waiting for dramatic experiences, but actively cooperating with the Spirit's gentle, persistent work.

The Holy Spirit—the divine breath that hovered over creation, inspired Scripture, empowered Jesus's ministry, and now indwells believers — desires to guide your meditation practice. He transforms it from a human discipline into a divine-human communion, where God's purposes unfold in and through you.

In the next chapter, we'll explore the Christian Meditation Framework — a practical structure for implementing the principles we've studied thus far. This framework will help you establish a sustainable meditation practice that engages your whole being—body, soul, and spirit—in communion with the triune God.

May the Holy Spirit guide you into ever-deepening communion with the Father through the Son, transforming you "from one glory to another" as you yield to His gentle, powerful presence.

# CHAPTER NINE:
# The Christian Meditation Framework

After exploring meditation's biblical foundations, scientific evidence, and spiritual dimensions, we now use a practical framework for implementing these insights into your daily life. The Christian Meditation Framework presented in this chapter provides a structured approach that honors biblical principles while addressing the practical realities of modern life. The core of this framework is the divine breath, God's Ruach and Neshama, which connects you to His presence and power in every moment.

## The Divine Breath: The Center of Christian Meditation

Before examining the specific components of the framework, let's establish the central role of breath in Christian meditation.

### The Breath as Sacred Connection

Your breath is a biological function and a sacred connection to your Creator. As you discovered in Chapter 5, the Hebrew words Ruach and Neshama reveal that your breathing carries profound spiritual significance.

- **Divine Origin**: Your breath originates from God Himself, who "**breathed into [Adam's] nostrils the breath of life" (Genesis 2:7)**.
- **Ongoing Sustenance**: Job affirms that **"the Breath (Neshama) of the Almighty gives me life" (Job 33:4)**—in the present tense, showing continuous divine nourishment.
- **Spiritual Presence**: Your breath carries God's holiness **(Resh)**, connects Heaven and Earth **(Vav)**, and binds you to God **(Cheth)**.
- **Transformative Power**: Through your breath flows God's divine wisdom, understanding, counsel, might, knowledge, and reverence (Isaiah 11:2).

When you consciously engage with your breath during meditation, you're not merely practicing a relaxation technique; you're reconnecting with the divine gift that animates your being and facilitates communion with Heaven and Earth.

## The Breath as Spiritual Anchor

Besides its theological significance, your breath serves as a practical anchor for meditation.

- **Always Present**: Unlike other meditation objects that may be unavailable in certain circumstances, your breath is always with you.
- **Continuously Rhythmic**: The natural rhythm of breathing provides a consistent pattern that helps to stabilize attention.

- **Physically Tangible**: The sensations of breathing offer concrete physical feedback that helps ground spiritual awareness.
- **Emotionally Responsive**: Your breath reflects and influences your emotional state, bridging body and spirit.
- **Spiritually Symbolic**: The inhalation-exhalation cycle symbolizes receiving from God and releasing to Him.

By centering your meditation practice on breath awareness, you establish a foundation that integrates body, soul, and spirit in communion with God.

## The Breath as Holy Spirit Conduit

Most significantly, conscious breathing facilitates a deeper connection with the Holy Spirit (Pneuma):

- **Linguistic Connection**: The Greek word Pneuma, like the Hebrew Ruach, means "breath" and "spirit. "
- **Incarnational Reality**: Your physical breathing becomes a tangible reminder of the Spirit's invisible presence.
- **Receptive Posture**: Breath awareness creates an inner openness that enhances receptivity to the Spirit's guidance.
- **Surrendered Control**: Conscious breathing involves a balance of intentionality and release that mirrors spiritual surrender.
- **Transformative Medium**: The Spirit works through your breath to bring peace, clarity, and divine presence.

As Jesus breathes on His disciples and says, **"Receive the Holy Spirit" (John 20:22**), your conscious breathing becomes a means of receiving more of the Spirit's presence and power in your life.

# Core Principles of Breath-Centered Christian Meditation

With the divine breath as our foundation, let's establish the core principles that distinguish Christian meditation from other approaches:

## 1. Christ-Centered Focus Through the Breath

Unlike meditation practices that aim at self-improvement or heightened consciousness as ultimate goals, Christian meditation is Christ-centered. Jesus Christ—His person, work, teachings, and presence—is our meditation's central focus. Your breath serves as the bridge that connects you to Christ's indwelling presence.

When distractions arise—as they inevitably will—your breath provides a consistent anchor to return to, redirecting your attention to Christ. With each inhalation, imagine receiving more of Christ's presence; release anything that separates you from Him with each exhalation. This breath-centered focus ensures that meditation serves its proper purpose: deepening your relationship with God rather than merely enhancing your psychological well-being (though this often occurs as a beneficial side effect).

## 2. Scripture-Guided Content Carried on the Breath

While Christian meditation may incorporate various elements, Scripture provides the authoritative content that guides and governs the practice. As the psalmist declares, **"Your word is a lamp for my feet, a light on my path" (Psalm 119:105**). Your breath becomes the carrier of this divine Word, bringing it from the page into your very being.

Try synchronizing your breathing with Scripture verses, inhaling as you receive God's truth, and exhaling as you release resistance. For example, breathe in while mentally reciting **"The Spirit of God has made me"** and breathe out while completing the verse, **"and the breath of the Almighty gives me life." (Job 33:4**). This practice integrates God's Word with the physical reminder of His sustaining presence in your life.

## 3. Spirit-Led Process Through Conscious Breathing

Christian meditation is not a self-directed technique, but a Spirit-led communion. The Holy Spirit—whom Jesus promises will "guide you into all the truth" (John 16:13)—actively takes part in the meditation process. Your conscious breathing creates space for the Spirit's guidance by calming mental chatter and emotional turbulence.

When you feel disconnected from the Spirit's guidance, return to your breath. As you breathe deeply and consciously, affirm that you are breathing in the very presence of God. This breath awareness helps you recognize the subtle promptings of the Spirit. Internal and external noise might otherwise drown that out.

## 4. Holistic Engagement Facilitated by the Breath

Biblical meditation engages the whole person—spirit, soul (mind, will, emotions), and body—in communion with God. This holistic approach reflects the biblical understanding of human nature and fulfills Jesus's command to **"love the Lord your God with all your heart and with all your soul and with all your mind and with all your strength." Mark 12:30 (NIV)**

Your breath naturally integrates these dimensions:

- **Body**: The physical sensations of breathing anchor you in bodily awareness.
- **Mind**: Focusing on breath calms mental activity and enhances clarity.
- **Emotions**: Breath regulation helps process and transform emotional states.
- **Spirit**: Breath awareness facilitates spiritual receptivity and communion.

Rather than attempting to escape the body or suppress emotions, breath-centered Christian meditation integrates all dimensions of your being in worship and communion.

## 5. Transformational Purpose Empowered by Divine Breath

The ultimate purpose of Christian meditation is transformation into Christ's likeness. Paul describes this process:

**"And we all, who with unveiled faces contemplate the Lord's glory, are being transformed into his image with ever-increasing glory, which comes from the Lord, who is the Spirit," 2 Corinthians 3:18 (NIV)**

Your breath serves as the vehicle for this transformation. With each breath cycle, you can:

- **Receive** God's holiness, wisdom, and power (inhalation)
- **Release** sin, fear, and resistance (exhalation)
- **Renew** your mind according to God's truth (complete breath cycle)
- **Realign** your will with God's purposes (rhythmic breathing)

This breath-centered approach to transformation recognizes that spiritual change occurs not through human striving but through surrendered receptivity to the Spirit's work.

## 6. Communal Connection Strengthened by Shared Breath

While often practiced individually, Christian meditation exists within the context of community. Faith community members should test and enrich the insights, experiences, and guidance gained from meditation. As Paul instructs, **"Let the message of Christ dwell among you richly as you teach and admonish one another with all wisdom through psalms, hymns, and songs from the Spirit, singing to God with gratitude in your hearts." Colossians 3:16 (NIV)**

Consider how breath connects you with the broader body of Christ:

[130]

- All believers breathe the same air, a physical reminder of our shared spiritual life.
- Corporate worship often involves synchronized breathing (as in singing)
- The Hebrew concept of Ruach applies both individually and communally.
- Jesus breathed on His disciples collectively, not just individually (John 20:22)

This communal dimension provides accountability and prevents meditation from becoming isolated or idiosyncratic.

# Creating Sacred Space and Time for Breath-Centered Meditation

The environment and timing of your meditation significantly affect its quality and effectiveness. While God is encounterable anywhere, anytime, creating a sacred meditation space and time intentionally facilitates deeper engagement and minimizes distractions.

## Physical Space Conducive to Breath Awareness

You don't need an elaborate space dedicated exclusively to meditation, but your meditation space should support focused attention and spiritual receptivity. Consider these elements:

## Location

Choose a quiet place with minimal interruptions and air quality that supports comfortable breathing. This might be a corner of your bedroom, a comfy chair in your study, or even a peaceful outdoor setting. Consistency in location helps condition your mind and body to enter a meditative state more readily.

## Seating

Select a comfortable position that supports an alert yet relaxed posture and allows unrestricted breathing. Traditional options include:

- Sitting in a straight-backed chair with feet flat on the floor.
- Kneeling with support (such as a meditation bench or cushion)
- Sitting cross-legged on a cushion or mat.
- Sitting with back supported against a wall.

The specific position matters less than finding one that allows you to breathe comfortably and remain alert for meditation.

## Visual Elements

Consider including simple visual elements that support spiritual focus without becoming distractions. These might include:

- A cross or other Christian symbol.

[132]

- A candle (representing Christ as the light of the world)
- A Bible or prayer book.
- Natural elements like plants or stones remind you of God's breath in creation.
- Artwork depicting biblical scenes or themes related to breath or spirit.

These elements should direct attention toward God rather than becoming objects of focus themselves.

## Minimizing Distractions

Reduce potential interruptions that might disturb your breath awareness by:

- Silencing electronic devices or placing them in another room.
- Informing household members of your meditation time.
- Addressing basic physical needs (hunger, thirst) beforehand.
- Keep a small notepad nearby to jot down intrusive thoughts or arising tasks quickly so you can return to breath meditation without fear of forgetting something important.

Remember Jesus's teaching about private prayer: **"But when you pray, go into your room, close the door, and pray to your Father, who is unseen." Matthew 6:6 (NIV)**

While this doesn't mandate a specific location, it emphasizes the value of privacy and freedom from distraction when communing with God through breath-centered meditation.

# Sacred Time for Breath Communion

When you meditate, it is as important as where you meditate. Consider these aspects of sacred time:

## 1. Frequency

Regular breath-centered practice yields greater benefits than occasional intensive sessions. Begin with a realistic commitment—perhaps 10-15 minutes daily—and gradually increase as the practice becomes integrated into your life. As the psalmist writes, **"Seven times a day I praise you" (Psalm 119:164)**, suggesting the value of regular spiritual practices throughout the day.

## 2. Timing

Identify times when you're naturally more alert, and your breathing is calm and receptive. Common options include:

- Early morning, before the day's activities begin.
- Midday, as a centering pause.
- Evening, as a transition from activity to rest.
- Before bedtime, as a preparation for sleep.

The specific time matters less than consistency and alignment with your natural breathing rhythms.

## 3. Duration

Start with a challenging but achievable duration—perhaps 10-20 minutes—and gradually extend as your capacity for sustained breath awareness increases. Quality matters more than quantity; a focused 15-minute breath meditation is more beneficial than a distracted 30-minute session.

## 4. Season

Recognize that different seasons of life may require adjustments to your breath meditation practice. During particularly busy or challenging periods, shorter, more frequent breath check-ins might be more sustainable than longer sessions. The biblical concept of the Sabbath reminds us that sacred time operates in cycles and seasons rather than rigid uniformity.

## 5. Preparation

Establish simple rituals that signal the transition into sacred time and prepare your breathing. These might include:

- Take three deep, conscious breaths.
- Reciting a brief prayer of invocation that acknowledges the divine origin of your breath.
- Reading a Scripture verse about God's breath or Spirit.
- Lighting a candle as a visual reminder of the Holy Spirit's presence.

These preparatory actions help shift attention from ordinary concerns to spiritual receptivity through the breath.

By thoughtfully creating sacred space and time for breath-centered meditation, you establish conditions conducive to meaningful communion with God. As Jesus withdrew to **"lonely places"** for prayer **(Luke 5:16**), you, too, can create set-apart contexts for breath communion with God, even amid a busy life.

# The Role of Scripture in Breath-Centered Meditation

Scripture forms the heart of Christian meditation, providing its content and authority. Unlike approaches emphasizing emptying the mind, biblical meditation involves filling the mind with God's truth and allowing it to transform your entire being. Your breath serves as the vehicle that carries this truth from the page into your heart.

Here are several ways to engage with Scripture through breath-centered meditation:

## 1. Breath-Synchronized Lectio Divina (Sacred Reading)

You can enhance this ancient practice through conscious breathing.

- **Lectio (Reading)**: Slowly read a short Scripture passage while breathing calmly and deeply. Notice which word or phrase captures your attention as you breathe.

- **Meditatio (Meditation)**: Synchronize your breathing with this word or phrase. Inhale as you receive its truth; exhale as you release resistance to it.
- **Oratio (Prayer)**: Allow your breathing to form a rhythm for your prayer response, perhaps inhaling God's truth and exhaling your response.
- **Contemplatio (Contemplation)**: Rest in God's presence, using your breath to anchor wordless communion.

This breath-centered approach to Lectio Divina honors Scripture's objective truth and the subjective experience of encountering God through His Word.

## 2. Scripture Memorization Through Breath Rhythms

Committing Scripture to memory provides internal resources for meditation throughout the day. Enhance this practice by:

- Synchronizing phrases with your breath rhythm.
- Inhalation and exhalation are used to divide verses naturally.
- Creating breath-based memory patterns (e.g., four keywords with four breaths)
- Reviewing memorized passages during regular breath check-ins throughout the day.

As you internalize biblical passages through breath-synchronized repetition, they become available for the Holy Spirit to bring to mind in various circumstances.

[137]

### 3. **For narrative passages, use your breath to enter the biblical story more fully**

- Breathe in the sights, sounds, and atmosphere of the scene.
- Let your breath match the emotional tone of the passage.
- Use breath awareness to place yourself physically within the story.
- Breathe with the biblical characters, imagining their emotional and spiritual states.

This approach, practiced by Ignatius of Loyola and many others throughout church history, helps Scripture move from abstract information to lived experience.

## 4. Thematic Breath Meditation

This approach involves selecting Scriptures related to breath, spirit, or a specific theme and meditating on them collectively:

- Gather verses about Ruach, Neshama, or Pneuma.
- Collect passages about God's sustaining presence.
- Focus on Scriptures that address your current spiritual needs.
- Create a breath prayer from each verse in your collection.

Thematic breath meditation helps connect individual verses to the broader biblical narrative and theological framework, preventing isolated or distorted interpretations.

## 5. Praying Scripture Through the Breath

Using biblical texts—especially Psalms—as the basis for breath-synchronized prayer:

- Inhale God's promises; exhale your trust.
- Breathe in God's attributes; breathe out your praise.
- Inhale God's commands; exhale your commitment.
- Breathe in God's comfort; breathe out your concerns.

This practice ensures that your prayers are shaped by divine truth rather than merely personal preferences or cultural influences.

## 6. Hebrew Letter Breath Meditation

This unique practice involves meditating on the meanings of the Hebrew letters in Ruach and Neshama:

- As you inhale, focus on receiving God's holiness (Resh)
- As you continue breathing, feel the connection between Heaven and Earth (Vav)
- As you complete your breath cycle, experience the binding with God (Cheth)
- With subsequent breaths, focus on the letters of Neshama: faith (Nun), wholeness (Shin), divine knowledge (Mem), and God's presence (Heh)

This practice deepens your appreciation for the spiritual treasures encoded in the biblical languages and connects you more intimately with the original revelation.

[139]

Whichever approach you choose, remember that the goal of Scripture meditation is not merely intellectual understanding, but a transformative encounter facilitated by the breath. As James writes, **"Do not merely listen to the word, and so deceive yourselves. Do what it says" (James 1:22).** Authentic Scripture meditation always moves toward application and obedience.

# Posture and Preparation for Breath-Centered Meditation

While the internal attitude matters more than external form, physical posture and preparation significantly influence the quality of your breath-centered meditation experience. The body is not an obstacle to spiritual practice, but a God-given instrument for worship and communion.

## Physical Posture for Optimal Breathing

The Bible mentions various prayer postures, including standing (Mark 11:25), kneeling (Ephesians 3:14), prostration (Matthew 26:39), and sitting (2 Samuel 7:18). This diversity suggests that no single posture is mandatory, but certain qualities enhance breath-centered meditation:

CHAPTER NINE:
The Christian Meditation Framework

Breathing Alignment

Choose a position that allows for full, unrestricted breathing. Your spine should be straight, your shoulders relaxed, and your chest open. This alignment permits deeper breathing and greater awareness of breath sensations.

## Stability for Sustained Breath Awareness

A stable position minimizes the need for adjustment during meditation, allowing you to maintain continuous breath awareness. Establish a foundation that can be kept for the intended duration, whether sitting, kneeling, or standing.

## Openness to the Breath of God

Physical openness often facilitates spiritual receptivity to God's breath. Consider uncrossing arms and legs, relaxing clenched hands, and adopting a posture that symbolizes openness to the Spirit's movement, like the disciples who gathered in the upper room, receptive to the rushing wind of Pentecost.

## Intentionality with Each Breath

Whatever posture you choose, adopt it intentionally as an expression of your spiritual purpose. With each breath, renew your intention to commune with God through this physical-spiritual connection.

Experiment with different positions to discover what best supports your breath-centered meditation practice, recognizing that physical needs and capabilities vary among individuals and may change.

## Mental Preparation Through Breath Awareness

Before beginning meditation, prepare your mind through breath-centered practices:

### Breath-Based Transition Ritual

Create a simple ritual centered on your breathing that signals the shift from ordinary activities to sacred attention. Take three deep, conscious breaths, perhaps saying silently with each cycle: "I am breathing in God's presence; I am releasing all distractions." This breath-centered transition helps the mind disengage from previous concerns and reorients toward spiritual receptivity.

### Breath-Aligned Intention Setting

Clarify your purpose for this meditation session while synchronizing with your breathing. As you inhale, receive God's purpose; as you exhale, release your agenda. This breath-aligned intention helps direct your attention without becoming rigid or demanding.

### Breath-Centered Expectancy

Approach meditation with hopeful expectancy rather than specific demands, using your breath as an anchor for this balanced attitude. Expect to encounter God with each breath, but release expectations about how that encounter should feel or what insights it should produce. As Jesus taught, **"Ask and it will be given to you; seek and you will find; knock and the door will be opened to you" (Matthew 7:7).**

[142]

**Breath-Acknowledge Distractions**

Before beginning, take a few moments to acknowledge likely distractions while breathing calmly. With each exhalation, mentally release these concerns, knowing you can return to them later. This breath-centered acknowledgment often reduces their power during meditation.

# Spiritual Preparation Through Divine Breath

Beyond physical and mental preparation, consider these breath-centered spiritual practices:

## Breath Invocation

Begin by explicitly inviting God's presence through a breath-synchronized prayer such as "Come, Holy Spirit" (inhale), "Fill me with Your presence" (exhale). This invocation acknowledges that meditation is not a self-generated experience but a response to a divine initiative carried on the breath.

## Breath Confession

Briefly acknowledge any known sin or resistance that might hinder communion with God, using your breath as a vehicle for confession. As you inhale, receive God's forgiveness; as you exhale, release the sin or resistance. This breath-centered confession creates spiritual openness.

## Breath Dedication

Offer the meditation time to God as an act of worship and love, using your breath as the symbol of this offering. As you breathe, affirm that each breath belongs to God and serves His purposes. This dedication transforms meditation from a self-improvement technique into a relational gift.

## Breath-Carried Scripture

Even if your meditation will not focus directly on a biblical text, begin with a breath-synchronized reading of a brief passage. Allow the words to flow with your breathing rhythm, centering your practice on God's revealed truth.

These preparatory elements need not be lengthy or elaborate. Even a few moments of intentional breath-centered preparation can significantly enhance the depth and focus of your meditation practice, creating conditions conducive to genuine communion with God.

# Overcoming Common Obstacles Through the Breath

Every meditation practice encounters obstacles. Rather than being discouraged by these challenges, view them as opportunities for growth and deepening commitment. Here are some common obstacles and breath-centered strategies for addressing them:

# 1. Distraction and the Anchoring Breath

Perhaps the most universal meditation challenge is mental distraction—the mind's tendency to wander from its intended focus to random thoughts, worries, plans, or memories.

**Biblical Perspective**: Jesus acknowledged the reality of distraction in His parable of the Sower, where the seed (God's Word) is choked by **"the worries of this life and the deceitfulness of wealth" (Matthew 13:22)**. Paul also recognized this challenge, urging believers to **"take captive every thought to make it obedient to Christ" (2 Corinthians 10:5)**.

**Breath-Centered Strategies**:

- Use your breath as a constant anchor to return to when distractions arise.
- Label distractions as "thinking" and gently return attention to your breath.
- Count breaths (1-10, then repeat) to strengthen concentration.
- Silently say "inhaling" and "exhaling" to reinforce breath awareness.
- When particularly distracted, take three intentionally deep breaths to reset your focus.
- Remember that your breath carries God's holiness, connecting Heaven and Earth with each cycle.

The breath is the most reliable tool for managing distractions because it is always present, rhythmic, and connected to physical and spiritual reality.

## 2. Dryness and the Enlivening Breath

**Spiritual dryness**—periods when God seems distant, and meditation feels mechanical—challenges even the most committed practitioners.

**Biblical Perspective**: The psalmist experienced this: "**My soul thirsts for God, for the living God. When can I meet with God?" (Psalm 42:2**). Jesus Himself cries out, **"My God, my God, why have you forsaken me?" (Matthew 27:46**), expressing the ultimate experience of spiritual dryness.

**Breath-Centered Strategies**:

- Remember that your breath continues even in dry seasons, just as God's presence remains, regardless of feelings.
- Focus on the physical sensations of breathing to stay grounded in present reality.
- Recall that the divine Neshama flows through your nostrils even when you don't feel it.
- Use breath visualization—perhaps imagining your breath as a bright light or living water.
- Breathe with the awareness that the Holy Spirit intercedes for you "with groans that words cannot express" (Romans 8:26)

The breath reminds you that spiritual life continues even in seasons of dryness, just as physical life continues through your breathing, regardless of how you feel.

## 3. Physical Discomfort and the Healing Breath

**Physical discomfort**—whether from a sitting position, health issues, or normal bodily sensations—can significantly distract during meditation.

In a Biblical context, Paul discussed his **"thorn in the flesh"** (2 Corinthians 12:7) and understood that God's **"power is perfected in weakness"** (2 Corinthians 12:9). The body, though subject to weakness and discomfort, remains the temple of the Holy Spirit (1 Corinthians 6:19).

**Breath-Centered Strategies**:

- Direct your breath mentally toward areas of discomfort, imagining God's healing presence flowing there.
- Adjust your position mindfully if necessary, maintaining breath awareness throughout the movement.
- Use discomfort as an opportunity to practice compassion toward your body through gentle breathing.
- Remember that Christ suffered physically and understands bodily limitations.
- Breathe with the awareness that your body will eventually be resurrected and perfected.

The breath is both a comfort in discomfort and a reminder that the Spirit dwells within your body, making it sacred despite its limitations.

## 4. Emotional Turbulence and the Calming Breath

**Powerful emotions**—anxiety, frustration, anger, sadness, and even excitement—can overwhelm meditation and make spiritual focus difficult.

**Biblical Perspective**: Jesus experienced the full range of human emotions, from anger (Mark 3:5) to grief (John 11:35) to joy (Luke 10:21). The Psalms demonstrate that emotional honesty is compatible with deep spirituality.

**Breath-Centered Strategies**:

- Allow your breath to acknowledge and express emotions rather than suppressing them.
- Practice longer exhalations than inhalations to activate the parasympathetic nervous system and calm emotional intensity.
- Name the emotion with each exhalation: "breathing out anxiety," "releasing anger."
- Recall that Ruach refers to both breath and emotional state, affirming the connection between breathing and feeling.
- Breathe with the awareness that the Holy Spirit is present in your emotional experience.

The breath provides a pathway through emotional turbulence, neither denying feelings nor being controlled by them, but bringing them into God's presence for transformation.

[148]

## 5. Spiritual Warfare and the Empowering Breath

Meditation sometimes encounters spiritual resistance or attacks, manifesting as unusually persistent distractions, oppressive thoughts, or a sense of spiritual heaviness.

**Biblical Perspective**: Paul acknowledges that **"our struggle is not against flesh and blood, but against the rulers, against the authorities, against the powers of this dark world and against the spiritual forces of evil in the heavenly realms." Ephesians 6:12 (NIV)**
Jesus faced direct spiritual opposition during His wilderness fast (Matthew 4:1-11).

**Breath-Centered Strategies**:

- Remember that your breath carries the power of the Holy Spirit greater than any opposing force.

- Breathe in God's protection; breathe out fear and intimidation.

- Synchronize Scripture declarations with your breathing: "Greater is He" (inhale) "that is in me" (exhale)

- Recall Isaiah 11:2—with each breath, you receive the Spirit of wisdom, understanding, counsel, might, knowledge, and reverence.

- Breathe with the awareness that Jesus has defeated the enemy through His death and resurrection.

The breath reminds you that you are not fighting for victory but from victory, as the same Spirit that raised Christ from the dead dwells in you (Romans 8:11).

Addressing these common obstacles through breath-centered approaches transforms challenges into opportunities for deeper spiritual growth and more consistent meditation practice.

# Integrating Breath-Centered Meditation into Daily Life

The ultimate goal of Christian meditation is not just to have meaningful meditation sessions, but to transform your entire life into an expression of Christ's presence. Breath awareness serves as the bridge between formal meditation and moment-by-moment spiritual consciousness.

## Breath Check-Ins Throughout the Day

Establish regular breath check-ins—brief moments of breath awareness that reconnect you with God's presence.

- Set reminders on your phone or computer.

- Associate breath awareness with routine activities (opening doors, washing hands, etc.)

- Practice a breath check-in at the top of each hour.

- Take three conscious breaths before meetings, meals, or transitions.

- Use waiting times (traffic lights, lines, music while on hold during phone calls) for breath communion.

These brief check-ins prevent you from spending extended periods in meditative unconsciousness and help maintain spiritual awareness throughout the day.

## Breath-Centered Response to Triggers

Identify emotional or situational triggers that typically cause you to react unconsciously and develop a breath-centered response:

- When feeling angry, take five deep breaths before speaking.

- When anxious, practice 4-7-8 breathing (inhale for 4, hold for 7, exhale for 8)

- When tempted, breathe while silently reciting a relevant Scripture.

- When criticized, breathe in acceptance and breathe out defensiveness.

- When overwhelmed, take a "breathing space" of 60-90 seconds.

This practice transforms reactive patterns into responsive choices aligned with the Spirit's guidance.

## Breath Prayers for Specific Contexts

Develop short-breath prayers tailored to different contexts and needs:

[151]

- **For work**: "Lord Jesus" (inhale), **"guide my work"** (exhale)

- **For relationships**: "Divine love" (inhale), **"flow through me"** (exhale)

- **For decisions**: "Holy Spirit" (inhale), **"grant wisdom"** (exhale)

- **For stress**: "Prince of Peace" (inhale), **"calm my heart"** (exhale)

- **For temptation**: "Spirit of God" (inhale), **"strengthen me"** (exhale)

These breath prayers provide spiritual resources for specific challenges while maintaining breath awareness throughout diverse circumstances.

## Breath-Synchronized Scripture Meditation

Select key verses to synchronize your breathing throughout the day:

- **"Be still"** (inhale), **"and know that I am God."** (exhale)Psalm 46:10

- **"The Lord is my shepherd,"** (inhale), **"I shall not want."** (exhale) - Psalm 23:1

- **"I can do all things,"** (inhale), **"through Christ who strengthens me."** (exhale) Philippians 4:13

- **"Cast all your anxiety,"** (inhale), **"on him because he cares for you."** (exhale) - 1 Peter 5:7

- **"The peace of God,"** (inhale), **"which transcends all understanding."** (exhale) - Philippians 4:7

This practice integrates Scripture, breath awareness, and daily activities into a seamless spiritual experience.

## Breath-Centered Examination of Consciousness

Use your breath to review your day with God at day's end.

- Breathe deeply to center yourself in God's presence.

- With each inhalation, recall a significant moment from your day.

- With each exhalation, offer that moment to God for insight and guidance.

- Breathe in gratitude for moments of faithfulness and grace.

- Breathe out a confession for moments of failure or resistance.

- Conclude with breath-synchronized thanksgiving and commitment.

This practice fosters spiritual growth through regular reflection and accountability.

Integrating breath awareness throughout your day transforms your life into an ongoing communion with God. The distinction between "meditation time" and "regular life" dissolves as you maintain meditative consciousness through the sacred gift of breath.

# Conclusion: The Breath-Centered Christian Life

The Christian Meditation Framework presented in this chapter provides a comprehensive approach to spiritual formation centered in the divine breath. By recognizing your breath as a sacred connection to God, a spiritual anchor, and a Holy Spirit conduit, you transform an automatic biological function into a continuous opportunity for divine communion.

This breath-centered approach to Christian meditation offers several unique advantages:

- **Accessibility**: Everyone breathes, making this practice available regardless of education, background, or circumstances.

- **Portability**: Your breath is always with you, allowing for meditation anywhere, anytime.

- **Integration**: Breath awareness naturally bridges body, mind, emotions, and spirit.

- **The Bible** firmly roots the breath-spirit connection in its revelations.

- **Transformative Power**: Conscious breathing facilitates the Spirit's work of inner transformation.

As you implement this framework, remember that the goal is not a perfect technique but a deepening relationship. The divine breath—Ruach, Neshama, Pneuma—is not an impersonal force but the very presence of the triune God, inviting you into moment-by-moment communion.

In the next chapter, we'll explore how this breath-centered meditation framework equips you for spiritual warfare, transforming it from an intimidating concept into a practical reality where you experience Christ's victory in your daily life.

May each breath you take become a reminder of God's sustaining presence and an opportunity for deeper communion with the One who breathed life into you and continues to empower you through His Spirit.

# CHAPTER TEN:
# Meditation For Spiritual Warfare

As we deepen our Christian meditation practice, we recognize that we're engaging in more than a personal spiritual discipline—we're taking part in a cosmic struggle between the kingdom of God and the forces opposing it. Scripture is clear: **"For our struggle is not against flesh and blood, but against the rulers, against the authorities, against the powers of this dark world and the spiritual forces of evil in the heavenly realms." Ephesians 6:12 (NIV)**

In this chapter, we'll explore how meditation equips us for this spiritual warfare, transforming it from an intimidating concept into a practical reality in which we experience Christ's victory in our daily lives.

## The Divine Breath as Spiritual Protection

Before we identify the battlegrounds of spiritual warfare, it's essential to understand how the divine breath—God's Ruach— serves as our first line of defense. When God formed Adam from the dust and breathed the breath of life (Neshama) into him, He established a protective boundary around human consciousness. This divine breath wasn't merely biological respiration, but a sacred infusion of God's presence that continues today.

The Hebrew letters of **Ruach (רוּחַ)** reveal this protective aspect: the **Resh (ר)** representing God's holiness, the **Vav (ו)** connecting heaven and earth, and the **Cheth (ח)** binding us to God. With each conscious breath, you reactivate this divine protection—drawing in God's holiness, reinforcing your connection to both physical and spiritual realms, and strengthening your covenant bond with the Creator.

This understanding transforms how you approach spiritual warfare. Your breath is not merely a calming technique, but a God-designed mechanism for establishing a protective boundary against spiritual attack. As you breathe consciously, you're not just managing anxiety; you're invoking the very presence of God that dispels darkness and establishes divine order, just as the Ruach of God hovered over the chaotic waters at creation (Genesis 1:2).

# Identifying Spiritual Battlegrounds

Spiritual warfare occurs on multiple fronts, some obvious and others subtle. Recognizing these battlegrounds is the first step toward engaging effectively in the struggle. As Jesus warned, "**Watch and pray so that you will not fall into temptation. The spirit is willing, but the flesh is weak**" **(Matthew 26:41**). This watchfulness requires discernment about where and how the battle manifests.

CHAPTER TEN:
Meditation For
Spiritual Warfare

## The Battlefield of the Mind

Paul identifies the mind as a primary battleground when he writes about **"arguments and every pretension that sets itself up against the knowledge of God and taking captive every thought to make it obedient to Christ" 2 Corinthians 10:5**. The enemy's strategy often involves planting thoughts contradicting God's truth—doubts about God's goodness, distortions of His character, deceptions about your identity, and discouragements about your purpose.

These thought patterns might include:

1. **Identity Lies**: "You're worthless," "You'll never change," "God couldn't love someone like you."
2. **Theological Distortions**: "God is angry with you," "You have to earn His favor," "Your sin is too great for grace."
3. **Hopelessness Thoughts**: "Nothing will ever change," "Your prayers don't matter," "You've failed too many times."
4. **Comparison Traps**: "Other Christians are more spiritual," "You should be further along by now," "Your struggles prove you're not truly saved."

These thoughts aren't random mental noise, but strategic attacks aimed at undermining your faith, hope, and love. Meditation equips you to recognize these thoughts as they arise, evaluate them against Scripture, and replace them with divine truth.

The breath of life provides a powerful tool in this mental battlefield. When invasive thoughts assault your mind, your conscious breath is an immediate anchor, creating a space between you and the thought. This space allows the Holy Spirit (Pneuma) to intervene with discernment. As you inhale, imagine drawing in God's truth; release the false thought as you exhale. This breath-centered discernment practice helps you distinguish between thoughts originating from your mind, God's Spirit, or opposing spiritual forces.

## The Battlefield of Emotions

While emotions are God-given aspects of being human, they can become battlegrounds when the enemy exploits them to drive behavior contrary to God's will. Scripture acknowledges this reality: **"In your anger, do not sin: Do not let the sun go down while you are still angry, and do not give the devil a foothold." Ephesians 4:26-27 (NIV)**

Emotional battlegrounds might include:

1. **Unforgiveness**: Holding onto resentment that festers into bitterness.
2. **Fear**: Allowing anxiety to prevent obedience to God's calling.
3. **Shame**: Believing the condemning voice rather than God's voice of acceptance.
4. **Despair**: Surrendering to hopelessness rather than clinging to God's promises.
5. **Pride**: Elevating self-sufficiency over dependence on God.

[159]

Meditation helps you develop emotional awareness—the ability to recognize emotions as they arise, understand their sources, and respond to them in alignment with God's truth rather than being controlled by them.

Here again, the divine breath offers a powerful intervention. When emotions threaten to overwhelm you, conscious breathing activates the parasympathetic nervous system, creating physiological calm for spiritual clarity. This isn't merely stress reduction—it's engaging the divine design of Neshama that connects your physical breathing to spiritual reality. As you breathe through intense emotions, you invite the Holy Spirit's calming presence to regulate your emotional state, fulfilling Jesus's promise: **"Peace I leave with you; my peace I give you" (John 14:27).**

## The Battlefield of Relationships

Jesus emphasized love for God and others as the greatest commandments (Matthew 22:37-40). This is showing that relationships are central to spiritual life—and therefore, prime targets in spiritual warfare. The enemy works to disrupt unity, foster division, and break down godly relationships.

Relational battlegrounds include:

1. **Church Disunity**: Conflicts, factions, and divisions within the body of Christ.
2. **Family Strife**: Breakdown in communication, trust, and love in marriages and families.

[160]

3.  **Isolation**: Withdrawal from the community that leaves believers vulnerable.
4.  **Unhealthy Soul Ties**: Relationships that pull believers away from God's purposes.

Meditation cultivates the self-awareness and God-consciousness necessary to recognize relational patterns that reflect spiritual attack rather than spiritual health.

The breath of life offers a profound relational dimension as well. When conflicts arise, conscious breathing reminds you that the same divine breath (Ruach) that animates you also animates the other person. This shared divine breath creates a spiritual connection that transcends disagreement. Before responding in conflict, take several conscious breaths, remembering that you're both bearers of God's image and recipients of His breath. This breath-centered perspective helps fulfill Paul's instruction to **"make every effort to keep the unity of the Spirit through the bond of peace" (Ephesians 4:3).**

## The Battlefield of the Body

Scripture affirms our bodies are temples of the Holy Spirit (1 Corinthians 6:19-20) and instruments to be yielded for righteousness (Romans 6:13). The enemy seeks to corrupt this temple and redirect these instruments toward destruction through various means:

1.  **Addictive Behaviors**: Substances or activities that create bondage.

2. **Physical Neglect**: Ignoring the body's need for rest, nutrition, and care.
3. **Sensual Indulgence**: Using the body for pleasure in ways that violate God's design.
4. **Health Idolatry**: Making physical perfection an ultimate concern.

Meditation helps integrate body, soul, and spirit, bringing physical existence under the lordship of Christ and recognizing the body as both a potential battleground and a God-given instrument for worship and service.

Your breath serves as the most immediate connection between your physical body and spiritual reality. When physical temptations arise, conscious breathing reminds you that your body's purpose transcends momentary pleasure; it's a vessel for God's Spirit. The Hebrew concept of Neshama reminds us that God's breath fills our physical bodies with divine purpose. When facing physical temptation, several slow, intentional breaths can reconnect you with this divine purpose, helping you **"honor God with your body" (1 Corinthians 6:20).**

By identifying these battlegrounds and applying breath-centered awareness to each, you become more alert to how spiritual warfare manifests in your life. Don't let this awareness create paranoia; instead, use it to cultivate strategic vigilance, as Peter advises: **"Be sober-minded; Your adversary the devil prowls around like a roaring lion, seeking someone to devour." 1 Peter 5:8 (ESV)**

# Meditation as Spiritual Armor

In **Ephesians 6:10-18**, Paul describes the **"full armor of God"** that equips believers for spiritual warfare. This armor isn't physical equipment but spiritual realities that protect and empower us in the cosmic struggle. Christian meditation helps us "put on" this armor not as a one-time action, but as a continuous state of spiritual readiness.

The divine breath is vital in activating and energizing each piece of spiritual armor. Just as physical armor requires proper breathing for effective movement in battle, spiritual armor functions optimally when empowered by a conscious connection to God's breath. As we explore each piece of armor, we'll see how breath-centered meditation enhances its protective and offensive capabilities.

## The Belt of Truth (Ephesians 6:14)

In Roman military attire, the belt held other armor in place, providing the foundation for carrying weapons. Similarly, truth serves as the foundation for spiritual warfare, keeping everything else together.

**Meditation Application**: Truth-centered meditation involves saturating your mind with Scripture, allowing God's reality to displace falsehood. When you meditate on biblical truth—about God's character, your identity in Christ, the finished work of the cross, the coming kingdom—you tighten the belt that holds your spiritual armor in place.

[163]

**Breath-Enhanced Practice**: Select a truth that directly counters a specific lie you're battling. For example, if struggling with worthlessness, meditate on **Ephesians 2:10: "For we are God's handiwork, created in Christ Jesus to do good works, which God prepared in advance for us to do."** As you inhale, silently repeat the first part ("For we are God's handiwork") as you exhale, complete the verse. This breath-synchronized Scripture meditation allows truth to penetrate more deeply, moving from intellectual assent to heart-level conviction as the divine breath carries God's word into your innermost being.

## The Breastplate of Righteousness (Ephesians 6:14)

The breastplate protected vital organs, particularly the heart. Righteousness—Christ's imputed righteousness and the practical righteousness that flows from it—protects our spiritual heart from enemy attacks.

**Meditation Application**: Righteousness-focused meditation involves both receiving Christ's righteousness through faith and aligning your actions with that righteous identity. When you meditate on your justified status before God and the Spirit's sanctifying work within you, you strengthen the breastplate that guards your heart.

**Breath-Enhanced Practice:** Begin meditation by consciously receiving Christ's righteousness as a gift, not an achievement. With each inhalation, imagine drawing in the righteousness of Christ, like a protective covering (Isaiah 61:10). With each exhalation, release any self-righteousness or performance

[164]

mentality. Then, examine one area of practical righteousness where you need growth, inviting the Holy Spirit (Pneuma) with each breath to transform your desires and actions in that area. This breath-centered approach acknowledges that righteousness comes not through human effort but through the indwelling Spirit, who empowers righteous living.

## Feet Fitted with Readiness from the Gospel of Peace (Ephesians 6:15)

Roman soldiers wore studded boots that provided stability in battle and enabled swift movement. Similarly, the gospel gives believers stability and mobility in spiritual warfare.

**Meditation Application**: Gospel-centered meditation involves rehearsing the good news of Christ's life, death, and resurrection, allowing it to ground you in unshakable peace while propelling you into mission. When you meditate on the gospel's implications for your life and the world, you prepare your feet to stand firm and advance God's kingdom.

**Breath-Enhanced Practice**: Meditate on a passage that encapsulates the power of the gospel (such as Romans 5:1-11 or 1 Corinthians 15:1-8). As you breathe deeply, feel your feet connecting firmly to the ground, symbolizing the stability the gospel provides. With each inhalation, receive the peace of God that **"transcends all understanding" (Philippians 4:7)**; with each exhalation, imagine this peace extending outward to others. This breath-centered stability prepares you both to stand firm in trials and to move forward in gospel mission, carrying God's peace wherever you go.

[165]

CHAPTER TEN:
Meditation For
Spiritual Warfare

## The Shield of Faith (Ephesians 6:16)

Roman soldiers' shields were large enough for full-body protection and could be linked for collective defense. Faith similarly protects believers individually and collectively from "the flaming arrows of the evil one."

**Meditation Application**: Faith-building meditation focuses on God's faithfulness, power, and promises rather than on circumstances, feelings, or apparent obstacles. When you meditate on who God is and what He has promised, you raise the shield that extinguishes doubt, fear, and accusation.

**Breath-Enhanced Practice**: Identify a specific "flaming arrow" currently assailing you—perhaps doubt, temptation, or accusation. Find Scriptures that directly counter this attack. As you inhale, imagine drawing God's truth into your being; as you exhale, visualize the shield of faith extinguishing the flaming arrow. For example, if battling condemnation, breathe in the truth of **Romans 8:1: "Therefore, there is now no condemnation for those who are in Christ Jesus,"** and breathe out any false guilt. This breath-synchronized faith practice acknowledges that faith the Holy Spirit (Pneuma) empowers it, whose very name connects to the breath of God.

## The Helmet of Salvation (Ephesians 6:17)

The helmet protected the head, the command center for the entire body. Past, present, and future salvation defend our minds from enemy attacks that undermine our security and hope in Christ.

CHAPTER TEN:
Meditation For
Spiritual Warfare

**Meditation Application**: Salvation-focused meditation involves contemplating the full scope of what Christ has accomplished and secured for you—justification (past), sanctification (present), and glorification (future). Meditating on these realities strengthens the helmet that guards your thought life from doubt and despair.

**Breath-Enhanced Practice**: Meditate on passages that address all three tenses of salvation, such as Titus 3:4-7 or Romans 8:29-30. With each breath cycle, focus on one aspect of salvation: Inhale while focusing on past justification ("I have been saved"), hold briefly while focusing on present sanctification ("I am being saved"), and exhale while concentrating on future glorification ("I will be glorified"). This breath-patterned meditation reinforces the comprehensive nature of salvation, protecting your mind from both past regrets and future anxieties by anchoring you in God's complete redemptive work.

## The Sword of the Spirit (Ephesians 6:17)

The sword was the only offensive weapon in the Roman soldier's arsenal. Similarly, the word of God—specifically, rhema, the spoken or applied word—is our offensive weapon in spiritual warfare.

**Meditation Application**: Word-wielding meditation involves not just reading Scripture but internalizing and applying it so thoroughly that you can speak it with authority in moments of spiritual attack. When you meditate on Scripture until it becomes part of you, you sharpen the sword that cuts through deception and darkness.

**Breath-Enhanced Practice**: Study how Jesus used Scripture during His wilderness temptation (Matthew 4:1-11). Notice that He didn't quote Bible verses but applied specific truths to temptations. Select Scriptures relevant to your battles and practice speaking to them aloud with authority. As you inhale, receive the word into your being; as you exhale, say it with conviction. This breath-empowered declaration recognizes the connection between the Spirit (Pneuma) and the breath, acknowledging that Scripture becomes a living sword when energized by the breath of God through your voice.

## Prayer in the Spirit (Ephesians 6:18)

While not technically a piece of armor, prayer "in the Spirit on all occasions" completes Paul's description of spiritual warfare equipment. Prayer connects us to God's power and guidance in battle.

**Meditation Application**: Spirit-led prayer meditation involves listening before and during prayer, allowing the Holy Spirit to guide your intercession beyond your limited understanding. When you meditate in receptive silence, attentive to the Spirit's promptings, you discover how to pray according to God's will rather than merely your perceptions.

**Breath-Enhanced Practice:** Begin prayer with silent, attentive breathing, recognizing that the same word (Pneuma/Ruach) means both "Spirit" and "breath" in biblical languages. This linguistic connection reveals a profound spiritual reality: your breath can become a tangible point of communion with the Holy Spirit. As you breathe slowly and deeply, surrender your prayer agenda and ask the Spirit to **"intercede for us through wordless groans" (Romans 8:26).**

When impressions, Scriptures, or insights arise, breathe them in fully before expressing them in prayer. This breath-synchronized intercession acknowledges that true prayer flows not from human effort, but from divine inspiration from God's breath.

By integrating these breath-enhanced, armor-focused meditations into your regular practice, you develop defensive protection and offensive readiness for spiritual warfare. Rather than putting on the armor as an occasional emergency measure, you learn to live armored—continuously clothed in the spiritual realities that ensure victory in Christ, empowered by the very breath of God that sustains your being.

Remember that the divine breath that fills your lungs is not merely biological respiration but the ongoing fulfillment of God's promise: **"I will put my Spirit in you and move you to follow my decrees" (Ezekiel 36:27).** Each conscious breath becomes an invitation for the Spirit's empowering presence in the spiritual battles you face, ensuring that you **"fight the good fight of the faith" (1 Timothy 6:12)** not through human strength but through divine power.

In the next chapter, we'll explore how meditation facilitates divine revelation—the reception of God's wisdom, guidance, and truth for specific circumstances and decisions. This dimension of meditation complements spiritual warfare by equipping you to resist evil and actively pursue God's purposes for your life.

# CHAPTER ELEVEN:
# Meditation For Divine Revelation

Throughout Scripture, God reveals Himself to His people through creation, His written Word, prophets and apostles, and ultimately, Jesus Christ. This divine revelation continues today as the Holy Spirit illuminates the truth, provides guidance, and deepens our understanding of God's character and purposes. In this chapter, we'll explore how Christian meditation creates the conditions for receiving divine revelation in ways that transform our lives and align us more fully with God's will.

## The Divine Breath as a Channel for Revelation

Before we explore specific meditation practices for divine revelation, it's essential to understand how the breath of life serves as a sacred channel for receiving God's wisdom and guidance. The Hebrew concept of **Neshama (נְשָׁמָה)**—the specialized divine breath explicitly given to humans—reveals a profound connection between our breathing and our capacity to receive divine revelation.

In **Job 32:8**, Elihu declares **"it is the spirit (Ruach) in a person, the breath (Neshama) of the Almighty, that gives**

**them understanding."** This verse reveals that the same divine breath that animates your physical body also enables spiritual understanding. Your capacity to receive divine revelation isn't merely a cognitive function but a gift embedded in God's breath into humanity.

This connection between breath and revelation appears throughout Scripture. When God breathed into Adam, he became physically alive and spiritually receptive, capable of walking with God in the garden and receiving divine communication. When Jesus appeared to His disciples after the resurrection, He breathed on them and said, "Receive the Holy Spirit" **(John 20:22),** connecting the divine breath with spiritual empowerment and insight.

As you prepare for meditation on divine revelation, recognize that each breath carries this revelatory potential. Your breathing isn't merely a biological function but a continuous reminder of your capacity to receive God's wisdom, guidance, and truth through the indwelling Holy Spirit (Pneuma)—the divine breath now living within you.

# Opening Your Heart to God's Voice

Divine revelation begins with receptivity—an open heart positioned to hear God's voice. Jesus repeatedly emphasized this receptivity with the phrase, **"Whoever has ears to hear, let them hear" (Matthew 11:15, 13:9, 13:43**). This suggests that while God is always speaking, we are not always listening with the attention that allows His voice to penetrate our consciousness and transform our lives.

Meditation cultivates this receptivity through several breath-centered practices:

## 1. Stillness Cultivation

**Psalm 46:10** instructs, **"Be still, and know that I am God."** This stillness isn't merely physical but encompasses mental, emotional, and spiritual quieting that creates space for God's voice to be heard above the noise of our own thoughts, feelings, and agendas.

**Breath-Enhanced Practice**: Begin your meditation with a period of intentional stillness, using your breath as a sacred anchor for attention. With each inhalation, receive the life-giving Ruach of God, with each exhalation, release distractions and mental noise. As thoughts arise, observe them without attachment and return to the rhythm of your breath. This isn't about emptying your mind, but about creating space for God to fill.

A helpful progression for this practice follows the pattern of Psalm 46:10, synchronized with your breathing: -

Inhale: **"Be still,"** Exhale: **"and know that I am God,"**–Inhale: **"Be still,"** Exhale: **"and know that I am,"**–Inhale: **"Be still,"** Exhale: **"and know"**–Inhale: **"Be still,"** Exhale: (silent release)–Inhale: **"Be still"**, Exhale: (rest in God's presence)– This breath-synchronized simplification helps quiet the analytical mind and open the contemplative heart where divine revelation is received. The progressive shortening of the phrase mirrors the journey from complex thought to simple awareness of God's presence, carried on the rhythm of your breath.

## 2. Expectant Listening

Habakkuk modeled expectant listening when he declares, "**I will stand at my watch and station myself on the ramparts; I will look to see what he will say to me." Habakkuk 2:1 (NIV)** ·This posture combines patience with anticipation—waiting for God to speak while confidently expecting that He will.

**Breath-Enhanced Practice**: After establishing stillness, transition to expectant listening by synchronizing your breath with receptivity. As you inhale, silently pray, "**Speak, Lord**;" as you exhale, complete the prayer, "**For your servant is listening**" (1 Samuel 3:9). Allow your breathing to create a rhythm of invitation and receptivity, neither passively drifting nor actively straining but attentively waiting like a servant anticipating the master's voice.

This breath-centered expectancy acknowledges that the same divine breath (Ruach) that fills your lungs is the Spirit who reveals God's truth. As Jesus promises, **"When he, the Spirit of truth, comes, he will guide you into all the truth" (John 16:13).** Your conscious breathing becomes a tangible reminder of this indwelling revelatory presence.

## 3. Heart Preparation

Jesus taught that the condition of our heart determines our capacity to receive divine revelation. In the sower's parable (Matthew 13:1-23), the same seed (God's word) produced dramatically different results depending on the soil (the human heart) where it fell.

**Breath-Enhanced Practice**: Before seeking divine revelation, use your breath as a tool for heart examination. With each inhalation, invite the Holy Spirit to search your heart; with each exhalation, release conditions that might hinder your receptivity:

- Inhale: "**Search me, O God**" — Exhale: "**and know my heart**" (releasing hardness)
- Inhale: "**Test me**" — Exhale: "**and know my anxious thoughts**" (releasing shallowness)
- Inhale: "**See if there is any offensive way in me**," — Exhale: "**and lead me in the way everlasting**," (releasing thorns)

This breath-synchronized prayer from Psalm 139:23-24 invites the divine breath (Neshama) to prepare your heart as good soil—receptive, deep, and uncluttered—where divine revelation can take root and produce abundant fruit. The breath serves as the prayer's vehicle and a reminder of God's life-giving presence within you.

## 4. Humble Surrender

James writes, "**God opposes the proud but shows favor to the humble" (James 4:6).** Pride—whether intellectual, spiritual, or moral—creates resistance to divine revelation, while humility creates receptivity.

**Breath-Enhanced Practice**: Begin meditation with a breath-centered prayer of surrender. As you inhale, receive God's wisdom; as you exhale, release your limited understanding. With each breath cycle, acknowledge your complete dependence on God's revelation. Allow your breathing to embody the posture described in **Psalm 131:1-2: "My heart is not proud, LORD, my eyes are not haughty... But I have calmed and quieted myself. I am like a weaned child with its mother." (NIV)**

This breath-synchronized surrender recognizes that true wisdom comes not from human intellect but from the divine breath (Neshama) that gives understanding (Job 32:8). Each breath becomes a physical reminder of your dependence on God for revelation, fostering the humility that creates receptivity to divine truth.

# Discerning God's Voice

Once you've cultivated receptivity, the next challenge is discernment—distinguishing God's voice from other voices that compete for your attention. Jesus says, **"My sheep, listen to my voice; I know them, and they follow me" (John 10:27)**, showing that believers can recognize divine communication, but this recognition requires practice and discernment.

Meditation develops this discernment through several breath-centered practices:

The Spectrum of Divine Communication

Scripture reveals God communicates to us in various ways, forming a spectrum from subtle to dramatic:

- **Scripture Illumination**: The Holy Spirit brings biblical truth to the mind or reveals deeper meaning in familiar passages.

- **Conscience Promptings**: Internal sense of rightness or wrongness aligned with biblical principles.

- **Wisdom Insights**: Sudden clarity about situations or decisions that align with godly wisdom.

- **Prophetic Impressions**: Mental images, words, or sensations communicating specific divine messages.

- **Dreams and Visions**: Visual or auditory experiences conveying divine truth during sleep or waking.

- **Angelic Visitations**: Encounters with heavenly messengers bearing divine communication.

- **Audible Voice**: Rare instances of God speaking audibly.

Most believers experience the more subtle forms of divine communication regularly, while the more dramatic forms occur less frequently and often in specific circumstances of need or calling.

Divine breath plays a crucial role across this spectrum. The Hebrew understanding of Ruach and the Greek concept of Pneuma connect breath with spirit, revealing that God's communication often comes through the same divine breath that sustains your life.

When Scripture speaks of the Spirit's **"still, small voice" (1 Kings 19:12),** it points to this exceptional breath-like quality of divine communication—gentle yet powerful, subtle yet transformative.

### Testing What You Receive

Not every thought, impression, or spiritual experience comes from God. Scripture instructs us to "test the spirits to see whether they are from God" (1 John 4:1) and to "test everything; hold fast to what is good" (1 Thessalonians 5:21).

**Breath-Enhanced Discernment Practice:** When you receive what seems to be divine communication, use your breath as a tool for discernment. With each inhalation, invite the Holy Spirit's discernment; with each exhalation, apply one of these biblical tests:

1. **Scripture Alignment**: Does it align with God's revealed truth within Scripture? (**Inhale**: receive discernment; **Exhale**: compare with Scripture).

2. **Christ Glorification**: Does it honor Jesus Christ as Lord? (**Inhale**: receive discernment; **Exhale**: examine Christ-centeredness.

3. **Spiritual Fruit**: Does it produce the fruit of the Spirit? (**Inhale**: receive discernment; **Exhale**: consider resulting fruit).

4. **Community Confirmation**: Does it resonate with mature believers? (**Inhale**: receive discernment; **Exhale**: consider godly counsel).

5. **Peace Presence:** Does it bring God's peace even if challenging? (**Inhale**: I receive discernment; **Exhale**: notice inner peace).

This breath-synchronized discernment acknowledges that the same divine breath (Pneuma) that inspires revelation also enables discernment.

As Paul writes, **"The person with the Spirit makes judgments about all things" (1 Corinthians 2:15)**. Your conscious breathing becomes a practical tool for engaging this Spirit-empowered discernment.

# Meditation Practices for Divine Revelation

With receptivity cultivated and discernment engaged, specific meditation practices can help you receive divine revelation in various areas of need. Each practice creates conditions where God's voice can be heard more clearly through the channel of the divine breath.

## Lectio Divina: Receiving Revelation Through Scripture

Lectio Divina ("divine reading") is an ancient practice of meditative Scripture engagement that moves beyond information gathering to transformative encounter. This practice recognizes that the Bible is not merely a historical document but "living and active" (Hebrews 4:12) — God's ongoing revelation to His people.

Breath-Enhanced Practice: Select a short Scripture passage (5-10 verses) and engage with it through four breath-synchronized movements:

1. **Lectio (Reading)**: Read the passage slowly, attentively, with your breath as a natural pacing guide. Inhale between phrases. Exhale as you read each phrase, allowing the words to be carried on your breath like the divine Ruach that inspired them.

2. **Meditatio (Meditation)**: Reflect deeply on the passage, noticing words or phrases that stand out. With each inhalation, draw these words deeper; with each exhalation, allow their true meaning to expand your understanding.

3. **Oratio (Prayer)**: Respond to God based on what you've received. Let your breathing become a dialogue— inhaling to receive God's word, exhaling to offer your response in prayer.

4. **Contemplatio (Contemplation)**: Rest in God's presence beyond words or thoughts. Allow your breathing to become a wordless communion with the divine

breath that inspired Scripture and now dwells within you.

This breath-synchronized approach to Scripture meditation acknowledges that the same divine breath (Ruach) that inspired the biblical authors continues to illuminate Scripture for believers today. As Paul affirms, **"All Scripture is God-breathed" (2 Timothy 3:16)**—a powerful reminder that your breathing can become a point of connection with God's revelatory breath.

## Listening Prayer: Receiving Guidance for Decisions

When facing decisions or seeking direction, listening prayer creates space for divine guidance. This practice acknowledges God's promise: **"I will instruct you and teach you how you should go; I will counsel you with my loving eye on you" (Psalm 32:8).**

**Breath-Enhanced Practice**: Begin by centering yourself through conscious breathing, recognizing that the divine breath (Neshama) within you "gives understanding" (Job 32:8). Then follow these breath-synchronized steps:

1. **Presentation**: Inhale God's wisdom; pause, exhale your question or decision. State the matter clearly but without demanding a specific answer.

2. **Surrender**: Inhale God's will; exhale your preferences. Release attachment to particular outcomes, praying, **"Not my will, but yours be done" (Luke 22:42).**

3. **Listening**: Inhale receptivity; exhale distractions. Create space for God's response, which may come as thoughts, impressions, Scripture, or other means.

4. **Confirmation:** Inhale discernment; pause, exhale testing. Apply the biblical texts to what you receive, seeking confirmation through Scripture, peace, and community.

This breath-centered approach recognizes that guidance often comes not through dramatic interventions but through the **"still, small voice" (1 Kings 19:12)** that resembles the gentle movement of breath. Your conscious breathing becomes a tangible reminder of the divine Pneuma who **"will guide you into all the truth" (John 16:13)**.

## Prophetic Meditation: Receiving Insight for Others

Scripture encourages believers to **"eagerly desire gifts of the Spirit, especially prophecy" (1 Corinthians 14:1)**, which Paul defines as speaking **"to people for their strengthening, encouraging and comfort" (1 Corinthians 14:3)**. Prophetic meditation cultivates receptivity to insights God may provide for others' benefit.

**Breath-Enhanced Practice**: When you are seeking to minister prophetically to others, use your breath as a channel for divine insight.

1. **Preparation: Inhale** God's love; **exhale** self-focus. Center yourself in God's heart for the person or group, releasing personal agendas or assumptions.

[182]

2.  **Invitation**: **Inhale** openness; **exhale** barriers. Invite the Holy Spirit to reveal what would strengthen, encourage, or comfort those you serve.

3.  **Reception**: **Inhale** attentiveness; **exhale** analysis. Notice impressions, Scriptures, images, or words that arise, receiving them without immediately judging or interpreting.

4.  **Discernment**: **Inhale** wisdom; **exhale** presumption. Test what you've received against Scripture and the character of Christ before sharing.

5.  **Communication**: **Inhale** clarity; **exhale** confusion. Share what you've received with humility, allowing recipients to test and apply it appropriately.

This breath-synchronized approach acknowledges the connection between the divine breath and prophetic revelation. In Ezekiel's vision of dry bones, God commands, **"Prophesy to the breath (Ruach)... breathe into these slain, that they may live" (Ezekiel 37:9).** This powerful image reveals how prophetic ministry partners with the divine breath to bring life and restoration.

## Dream Reflection: Receiving Revelation During Sleep

Throughout Scripture, God frequently communicated through dreams to Jacob, Joseph, Daniel, and many others. While not every dream carries divine significance, Scripture affirms that **"God speaks — now one way, now another— though no one perceives it. In a dream, in a vision of the night..." (Job 33:14-15).**

# CHAPTER ELEVEN:
## Meditation For
## Divine Revelation

**Breath-Enhanced Practice**: To cultivate receptivity to divine revelation through dreams, establish this breath-centered routine:

1.  **Evening Preparation**: Before sleep, spend a few minutes in breath-centered prayer. As you inhale, invite God's communication; as you exhale, release the day's concerns. This creates spiritual receptivity during sleep.

2.  **Morning Recollection**: Upon waking, before rising, take several conscious breaths to maintain the liminal state between sleep and wakefulness where dream memory is strongest. With each inhalation, gather dream fragments; with each exhalation, bring them into conscious awareness.

3.  **Reflective Journaling**: Record significant dreams while maintaining breath awareness. Invite divine insight about the dream; write what comes to mind with each exhalation without censoring or analyzing.

4.  **Discernment Application**: Apply the biblical tests to dream content, using breath as a discernment tool. Inhale the Spirit's guidance, exhale personal interpretation or wishful thinking.

This breath-centered approach recognizes the intimate connection between sleep, breath, and divine communication. When God formed Adam and breathes the breath of life (Neshama) into him, Adam became a "living soul" (Genesis 2:7, KJV)—a being capable of receiving divine revelation even during sleep. Even as you sleep, your breathing maintains this connection to the divine breath that enables revelation.

## Integrating Revelation into Life

God intends divine revelation not merely for information or experience, but for transformation and action. James warns against being **"merely listeners to the word" rather than "doers" (James 1:22-25),** comparing those who receive a revelation without application to people who look at themselves in a mirror and immediately forget what they look like.

# Journaling: Recording and Processing Revelation

God instructed Habakkuk, **"Write down the revelation and make it plain on tablets" (Habakkuk 2:2**). Similarly, you record what you receive through meditation, creating a tangible record that facilitates reflection, application, and accountability.

**Breath-Enhanced Practice**: Establish regular journaling practice synchronized with your breathing.

1. **Centering**: Begin with several conscious breaths, connecting with the divine breath (Ruach) that enables understanding.

2. **Recording**: Write what you've received in meditation, allowing your natural breathing rhythm to pace your writing. Don't rush or force; let insights flow with your breath.

3. **Reflecting**: Pause periodically for deeper breaths, creating space to reflect on your writing. Ask breath-centered questions: "As I inhale God's truth, what more do I need to understand? As I exhale my response, how am I being called to apply this?

4.  **Responding:** Conclude with breath-synchronized prayer, inhaling God's empowerment and exhaling your commitment to obedience.

This breath-centered journaling acknowledges that the divine breath reveals truth and empowers its application. As Ezekiel prophesied to the dry bones, **"I will put breath in you, and you will come to life" (Ezekiel 37:6)**. Similarly, the revelations you record come to life through Spirit-empowered application.

# Community Discernment: Testing Revelation Together

Scripture emphasizes the communal dimension of revelation and discernment. Paul instructs that "the spirits of prophets are subject to the control of prophets" (1 Corinthians 14:32) and that prophecies should be "weighed carefully" by the community (1 Corinthians 14:29).

**Breath-Enhanced Practice**: When sharing revelations with trusted believers for spiritual discernment, incorporate breath awareness:

1.  **Humble Presentation**: Share what you've received while maintaining conscious breathing to remain grounded in humility. **Inhale** openness; **exhale** defensiveness.

2.  **Attentive Listening**: Receive others' discernment with breath-centered presence. Inhale their perspective, exhale resistance or justification.

3. **Unified Discernment**: Breathe together as a community seeking God's truth. This shared breathing symbolizes the one Spirit (Pneuma) who guides all believers into truth.

4. **Consensus Recognition:** Notice when peaceful agreement emerges, often accompanied by a collective sense of "breathing easier" as the Spirit confirms truth to the community.

This breath-aware communal discernment acknowledges that all believers share in the divine breath. At Pentecost, the Spirit came **"like the blowing of a violent wind" (Acts 2:2),** filling all believers and enabling them to participate in God's revelatory work. Your breathing in community becomes a reminder of this shared empowerment for discernment.

# Obedient Action: Responding to Revelation

Jesus emphasized that revelation must lead to obedience: **"Therefore, everyone who hears these words of mine and puts them into practice is like a wise man who built his house on the rock." Matthew 7:24 (NIV)** This Divine revelation always invites a response.

**Breath-Enhanced Practice**: When moving from revelation to action, use your breath to empower obedience.

1. **Clarity Confirmation**: Inhale God's wisdom; exhale confusion. Ensure you understand what specific action the revelation requires.

2.  **Courage Building**: Inhale God's strength; exhale fear. Draw on the power of the divine breath to overcome hesitation or resistance.

3.  **Commitment Making**: Inhale God's faithfulness; exhale self-reliance. Commit to obedience while recognizing your dependence on God's empowering presence.

4.  **Consistent Implementation**: Let's maintain breath awareness during action, inhaling God's guidance and exhaling your agenda. This breath-centered obedience keeps you aligned with the revelation's true intent.

This breath-synchronized obedience recognizes that the same divine breath that reveals truth also empowers its application. When Jesus breathes on His disciples and says, **"Receive the Holy Spirit" (John 20:22),** He connected the divine breath with empowerment for mission. Your conscious breathing during obedient action maintains this connection, allowing revelation to bear fruit in transformed living.

# Conclusion: The Continuous Breath of Revelation

As we conclude our exploration of meditation for divine revelation, remember that the breath of life flowing through you right now is not merely biological respiration, but a continuous connection to the God who reveals Himself to those who seek Him. Each breath you take carries the potential for divine communication—whether subtle promptings of conscience, illumination of Scripture, guidance for decisions, or prophetic insights for others.

# CHAPTER ELEVEN:
## Meditation For
## Divine Revelation

The Hebrew understanding of Neshama and the Greek concept of Pneuma reveal God has designed your breathing as a channel for His revelatory presence. This isn't mystical imagination but biblical reality—the same divine breath that first animated humanity continues to inspire, guide, and transform those who cultivate receptivity through meditation.

As you develop your meditation practice, let each conscious breath remind you of Jesus's promise: "When the Spirit of truth comes, he will guide you into all the truth" (John 16:13). The divine breath within you is not silent but speaking, not distant but intimately present, not stagnant, but continuously revealing God's heart and purposes for your life.

In the next chapter, we'll explore how meditation facilitates healing and restoration, addressing wounds, traumas, and brokenness through the therapeutic power of God's presence and truth. This healing dimension complements the revelatory aspect of meditation, as divine truth illuminates the mind and restores the heart.

**CHAPTER TWELVE:**
# Meditation for Healing And Restoration

Throughout Scripture, God reveals Himself as the healer of His people, not just physically, but emotionally, mentally, and spiritually. David proclaims, **"Praise the LORD, my soul, and forget not all his benefits—who forgives all your sins and heals all your diseases, redeems your life from the pit and crowns you with love and compassion." Psalm 103:2-4 (NIV)** This comprehensive healing is available to believers today, and Christian meditation provides a powerful pathway for experiencing this divine restoration.

## The Divine Breath as Healing Agent

Before exploring specific meditation practices for healing, it's essential to understand how the breath of life serves as a divine healing agent. In **Genesis 2:7**, when God **"breathed into [Adam's] nostrils the breath of life,"** He established a profound connection between the divine breath (Neshama) and human wholeness. This wasn't merely biological animation but the impartation of God's life-giving, healing presence.

Throughout Scripture, breath and healing are intimately connected. In Ezekiel's vision of the valley of dry bones, God commands, **"I will make breath enter you, and you will come to life" (Ezekiel 37:5).** This prophetic image reveals how the divine breath restores what is lifeless and broken. Similarly, when Jesus healed, He often used breath-related actions—speaking words (breath carrying sound), touching (requiring proximity of breath), and in one instance, even breathing on His disciples to impart the Holy Spirit (John 20:22).

The Hebrew letters of **Ruach (רוּחַ)** reveal this healing dimension: the **Resh (ר)** representing God's holiness that purifies, the **Vav (ו)** connecting heaven and earth to restore divine order, and the **Cheth (ח)** binding us to God in a covenant relationship where healing flows. With each conscious breath, you draw in God's purifying holiness, restore what was separated, and bind yourself to the Healer's covenant, thus engaging His divine healing presence.

As you approach meditation for healing, recognize that your breath isn't merely a relaxation technique but a sacred connection to the divine Healer. Each breath carries the potential for restoration, as you inhale God's healing presence and exhale brokenness, pain, and disease. This understanding transforms meditation from a coping mechanism into a genuine encounter with Yahweh Rapha—the Lord who heals.

# Understanding Holistic Biblical Healing

Before exploring specific meditation practices for healing, it's essential to understand the holistic nature of biblical healing. Unlike compartmentalized approaches that separate physical, emotional, and spiritual healing, Scripture presents an integrated view where all dimensions of human brokenness fall under God's redemptive work.

## The Biblical Concept of Shalom

The Hebrew word shalom, often translated simply as "peace," conveys a much richer concept of comprehensive well-being— wholeness in every dimension of existence. When God promises shalom to His people, He's offering complete restoration of what sin, suffering, and brokenness have damaged.

This holistic understanding appears throughout Scripture:

- In **Exodus 15:26**, God reveals Himself as **"the LORD, who heals you"** (Yahweh Rapha), addressing physical ailments within the context of the covenant relationship.
- In **Psalm 147:3**, God **"heals the brokenhearted and binds up their wounds,"** addressing emotional and psychological suffering.
- In **Isaiah 53:5**, the Messiah's suffering brings healing: **"by his wounds we are healed,"** addressing the spiritual brokenness caused by sin.
- James 5:14-16 shows a connection between prayer for the sick and confession of sin, recognizing a potential relationship between spiritual and physical conditions.

This integrated view doesn't mean that all suffering results directly from personal sin (Jesus explicitly rejected this simplistic view in John 9:1-3). However, it recognizes that all human brokenness stems from living in a fallen world and requires God's redemptive intervention.

The divine breath (Ruach) is central to this holistic healing. Just as God's breath initially integrated body, soul, and spirit in perfect harmony at creation, the restoration of that breath through conscious connection reintegrates what has been fragmented by sin and suffering. When you engage in breath-centered meditation, you're not just addressing symptoms but inviting God's original design of wholeness to be restored—the comprehensive shalom that encompasses every dimension of your being.

## Christ's Model of Holistic Healing

Jesus's healing ministry demonstrates this holistic approach. Consider these examples:

1.  **The Paralytic (Mark 2:1-12)**: Jesus addresses both spiritual need ("Your sins are forgiven") and physical condition ("Get up, take your mat and go home").

2.  **The Woman with Bleeding (Mark 5:25-34)**: Jesus provides physical healing and addresses social and spiritual dimensions by publicly acknowledging her and saying, "Daughter, your faith has healed you. Go in peace and be freed from your suffering."

3.  **The Gerasene Demoniac (Mark 5:1-20)**: Jesus heals not just spiritual oppression but also the man's psychological state, leaving him "dressed and in his right mind."

4.  **The Blind Man at Bethsaida (Mark 8:22-26)**: Jesus heals progressively, with partial restoration before complete healing, demonstrating that healing sometimes occurs in stages rather than instantaneously.

These examples reveal that Christ's healing addressed the whole person—body, mind, emotions, spirit, and social connections. This same holistic healing remains available to believers today, though it may manifest differently in different circumstances and often unfolds as a process rather than an instantaneous event.

The Holy Spirit (Pneuma) empowered Jesus's healing ministry—the divine breath that descended upon Him at His baptism. Luke records that "Jesus returned to Galilee in the power of the Spirit" (Luke 4:14) before beginning His healing ministry. This connection between the divine breath and healing power continues for believers today, as the same Spirit that empowered Christ now dwells within you, making your breath a potential channel for His healing presence.

## The Role of Meditation in Healing

Christian meditation facilitates healing by creating space for God's restorative presence to address our deepest wounds and brokenness. Unlike techniques focused solely on symptom management, meditation from a Christian perspective invites the Healer Himself to work within us, bringing transformation from the inside out.

# CHAPTER TWELVE:
## Meditation for Healing
## And Restoration

Meditation contributes to healing through several breath-centered mechanisms:

1.  **Presence Awareness**: Breath-centered meditation cultivates awareness of God's healing presence, allowing us to experience the truth that **"the LORD is close to the brokenhearted and saves those who are crushed in spirit" (Psalm 34:18).** Each conscious breath becomes a tangible reminder of this divine presence.

2.  **Truth Encounter**: Breath-synchronized meditation on Scripture brings God's truth into direct contact with the lies, distortions, and false beliefs that often underlie emotional and spiritual wounds. The divine breath carries this truth deep into your being.

3.  **Emotional Processing**: Conscious breathing during meditation creates safety for acknowledging and processing painful emotions in God's presence, fulfilling the invitation to **"cast all your anxiety on him because he cares for you" (1 Peter 5:7).**

4.  **Physiological Regulation**: The breath-body connection activates the parasympathetic nervous system, reducing stress hormones and creating physiological conditions conducive to healing. This isn't merely biological but a divine design that connects your breathing to your overall well-being.

5. **Spiritual Receptivity**: Breath-aware meditation opens your spirit to receive the healing ministry of the Holy Spirit, who **"helps us in our weakness" (Romans 8:26)** and applies Christ's finished work to our areas of need.

Engaging these mechanisms through breath-centered meditation creates optimal conditions for experiencing God's healing work in every dimension of your being. The divine breath that first made you whole at creation becomes the channel through which restoration flows in your present need.

# Meditation Practices for Physical Healing

While Scripture affirms God's power to heal physically— sometimes instantaneously and miraculously—it also reveals that physical healing often involves processes, means, and varying timelines according to God's wisdom. Meditation supports physical healing not by manipulating God, but by creating receptivity to His healing work through direct intervention, medical means, or the body's God-designed healing mechanisms.

## Breath as Life-Force Meditation

Scripture connects breath with physical life and vitality. Job acknowledges, **"The Spirit of God has made me the breath of the Almighty gives me life" (Job 33:4)**. This connection between divine breath and physical vitality provides the foundation for meditation that supports physical healing.

## CHAPTER TWELVE:
## Meditation for Healing
## And Restoration

**Breath-Enhanced Practice**: Find a comfortable position to breathe deeply without restriction. Place one hand on your chest and the other on your abdomen to feel the movement of breath. Then:

1.  **Awareness**: Begin by observing your natural breathing pattern without attempting to change it. Notice the sensation of air entering and leaving your body, recognizing this as the continuous gift of God's life-giving breath (Neshama).

2.  **Deepening**: Gradually allow your breathing to deepen, filling your lungs more completely with each inhalation and releasing more fully with each exhalation. Imagine the divine breath flowing into every cell of your body, carrying life, energy, and healing.

3.  **Directing**: If addressing a specific physical condition, gently direct your attention to that area as you breathe. With each inhalation, imagine God's healing breath (Ruach) flowing into that area, releasing tension, pain, or disease with each exhalation. This isn't visualization alone but conscious cooperation with the divine breath that "gives life to your mortal bodies" (Romans 8:11).

4.  **Receiving**: As you continue breathed deeply, silently pray, "Lord, I receive Your healing breath." Surrender to God's timing and method while maintaining faith in His healing presence flowing through your breath.

# CHAPTER TWELVE:
## Meditation for Healing
## And Restoration

This practice recognizes that your physical body was designed to be animated and sustained by God's breath. Each conscious breath reconnects you with this divine life-force, creating optimal conditions for physical healing according to God's will and timing.

## Scripture-Anchored Healing Meditation

God's word carries healing power, as He declares, **"I am the LORD, who heals you" (Exodus 15:26)** and **"He sent out his word and healed them" (Psalm 107:20).** Meditating on healing Scriptures allows these truths to penetrate your physical being through the vehicle of the divine breath.

**Breath-Enhanced Practice**: Select Scriptures that speak to God's healing nature and promises. Then:

1.  **Preparation**: Begin with several minutes of deep, conscious breathing, recognizing the connection between the divine breath and God's healing word.

2.  **Proclamation**: Read a healing Scripture aloud, allowing your breath to carry the words. For example, "By His wounds I am healed" (based on Isaiah 53:5).

3.  **Internalization**: Close your eyes gently and continue breathing deeply. With each inhalation, silently repeat the first part of the Scripture; with each exhalation, complete it. For example, **Inhale**: "By His wounds" — **Exhale**: "I am healed."

4. **Embodiment**: As you continue this breath-synchronized meditation, allow the Scripture to move from your mind to your heart and throughout your body. Imagine each cell receiving this truth carried on the divine breath.

This practice acknowledges that God's word and breath work together in healing. Just as God spoke creation into existence while His Spirit (Ruach) hovered over the waters, your spoken proclamation of Scripture, combined with conscious breathing, creates a powerful environment for physical restoration.

## Gratitude-Focused Body Meditation

Scripture encourages thanksgiving in all circumstances (1 Thessalonians 5:18) and reveals that gratitude creates an atmosphere conducive to healing. Jesus often thanked before performing healings, demonstrating the connection between gratitude and divine power.

**Breath-Enhanced Practice**: Sit or lie in a comfortable position and:

1. **Centering**: Begin with several deep breaths, connecting with the divine breath that sustains your physical body.

2. **Scanning**: Slowly scan your body from head to toe, paying attention to each part. As you focus on each area, breathe deeply into it.

3. **Thanking**: For each properly functioning part, inhale God's goodness and exhale gratitude: "Thank You,

Lord, for my functioning lungs." For areas needing healing, inhale God's faithfulness and exhale trust: "Thank You, Lord, that You are healing my joints."

4.  **Culminating**: Conclude with whole-body gratitude, breathing deeply as you thank God for the gift of your physical body as the temple of His Spirit (1 Corinthians 6:19-20).

This practice transforms your relationship with your physical body from criticism or frustration to gratitude and trust. The combination of conscious breathing and thanksgiving creates receptivity to the healing work of the divine breath (Ruach) that originally formed your body and continues to sustain it.

# Meditation Practices for Emotional Healing

Emotional wounds—whether from trauma, loss, rejection, or other painful experiences—often run deep and resist superficial solutions. Scripture acknowledges the reality of emotional suffering while pointing to God's healing presence: **"He heals the brokenhearted and binds up their wounds" (Psalm 147:3)**. Meditation creates space for this divine healing to reach the emotional layers of our being.

## Safe Haven Breath Meditation

Experiences that violated safety cause many emotional wounds. Scripture presents God as a refuge — **"God is our refuge and strength, an ever-present help in trouble."**

# CHAPTER TWELVE:
## Meditation for Healing
## And Restoration

**Psalm 46:1 (ESV)** This meditation helps establish an internal sense of safety in God's presence through the vehicle of the divine breath.

**Breath-Enhanced Practice**: Find a quiet place where you won't be disturbed and:

1. **Safety Establishment**: Begin with slow, deep breathing, imagining each breath surrounding you with God's protective presence. Silently repeat with each breath cycle: **"The name of the LORD is a fortified tower; the righteous run to it and are safe" (Proverbs 18:10).**

2. **Wound Acknowledgment**: As you continue breathing deeply, gently bring awareness to an emotional wound, noticing any sensations, feelings, or memories that arise. If the experience becomes overwhelming, return focus to your breath as an anchor.

3. **Divine Invitation**: Inhale God's compassionate presence; exhale the invitation, **"Lord, enter this wounded place."** Continue breathing as you allow God's healing breath (Ruach) to flow into this emotional wound.

4. **Comfort Reception**: With each inhalation, receive the comfort of the Holy Spirit (Pneuma), the "Comforter" Jesus promises. With each exhalation, release pain into God's hands. Continue this breathing pattern, allowing God's comfort to replace the emotional wound.

This practice creates a safe container for emotional healing through the consistent rhythm of the divine breath. Just as a mother's steady heartbeat and breathing calm a distressed child, your conscious connection to God's breath provides safety for acknowledging and healing emotional wounds.

## Breath-Centered Forgiveness Meditation

Unforgiveness often underlies persistent emotional pain. Jesus emphasized forgiveness as essential for spiritual health and taught His disciples to pray, "**Forgive us our debts, as we also have forgiven our debtors" (Matthew 6:12)**. This meditation facilitates the forgiveness process through breath awareness.

**Breath-Enhanced Practice**: Sit comfortably with spine erect and:

1. **Grace Reception**: Focus on God's forgiveness toward you. With each inhalation, receive God's unconditional forgiveness, with each exhalation, release shame and self-condemnation. Continue until you sense God's grace filling you.

2. **Wound Identification**: Bring to mind a person who has wounded you. As you breathe deeply, acknowledge the hurt without minimizing it. Remember that the same divine breath (Neshama) that gives your life also gives life to this person, creating a sacred connection despite the wound.

3. **Release Breathing**: Inhale God's perspective; exhale your right to revenge. Inhale God's healing; exhale the poison of bitterness. Inhale God's timing; exhale your

demand for justice now. Continue this pattern, allowing the divine breath to carry away the burden of unforgiveness.

4. **Blessing Intention**: As an ultimate step, breathe in God's love for the person who wounded you; breathe out a blessing upon them. This doesn't deny the wrong but releases it to God while choosing to align with His redemptive purposes.

This practice recognizes forgiveness not as a one-time decision, but as a process facilitated by the divine breath. Each breath cycle becomes an opportunity to release grievances and receive grace, fulfilling Jesus's teaching that we forgive "seventy-seven times" (Matthew 18:22)—a continuous process rather than a limited number.

## Emotional Regulation Through Breath Awareness Meditation

Intense emotions can overwhelm our capacity for a healthy response. Scripture acknowledges this reality while pointing to divine help: **"Cast all your anxiety on him because he cares for you" (1 Peter 5:7).** This meditation develops emotional regulation through conscious connection with the divine breath.

**Breath-Enhanced Practice**: This practice can be used whenever emotional intensity threatens to overwhelm:

1. **Recognition**: Notice the emotional intensity arising. Acknowledge its presence while focusing on your

breathing rather than suppressing or being controlled by it.

2.  **Rhythm Establishment**: Intentionally slow and deepen your breathing. Inhale to a count of four, hold briefly, exhale to a count of six. This longer exhalation activates the parasympathetic nervous system, creating physiological calming.

3.  **Divine Remembrance**: As you continue this breathing pattern, remember that your breath connects you to God's presence. Silently pray with each breath cycle: Inhale: "**The LORD is near**" — Exhale: "**to the brokenhearted**" (from Psalm 34:18).

4.  **Emotion Integration**: Once the intensity has reduced, inhale acceptance of the emotion as information; exhale resistance to feeling it. Inhale God's perspective on the situation; exhale your limited view. This breath-centered integration allows emotions to inform rather than control your response.

This practice doesn't deny emotional reality, but creates space between stimulus and response through the sacred rhythm of breath. The divine breath (Ruach) that hovered over chaos at creation brings similar order to emotional chaos, fulfilling God's promise: "I will give you a new heart and put a new spirit in you" (Ezekiel 36:26).

# Meditation Practices for Spiritual Healing

Spiritual wounds—whether from sin, religious trauma, disappointment with God, or spiritual warfare—affect our core identity and relationship with God. Scripture reveals God's desire to heal these deepest wounds: **"Return to me, and I will return to you" (Malachi 3:7)**. Meditation creates space for this spiritual restoration.

## Breath of Repentance and Renewal

Sin creates separation from God that requires healing through repentance and forgiveness. Scripture promises, **"If we confess our sins, he is faithful and just and will forgive us our sins and purify us from all unrighteousness" (1 John 1:9).** This meditation facilitates this spiritual cleansing through breath awareness.

**Breath-Enhanced Practice**: Find a private space where you can speak freely and:

1. **Examination**: Begin with slow, deep breathing, inviting the Holy Spirit to search your heart. With each exhalation, ask, "Lord, show me where I have grieved Your Spirit." Allow convictions to arise naturally without forcing or suppressing.

2. **Confession:** As specific sins come to mind, use your breath for confession. Inhale God's holiness; exhale specific acknowledgment: "Lord, I confess my pride in how I treated my colleague." Continue this breath-

confession pattern for each sin the Spirit brings to mind.

3. **Receiving Forgiveness**: After confession, shift to receiving forgiveness. With each inhalation, breathe in the truth: **"The blood of Jesus purifies me from all sin" (1 John 1:7).** With each exhalation, release shame, guilt, and self-condemnation.

4. **Renewal Commitment**: Conclude with breath-centered commitment to new patterns. Inhale God's empowering presence; exhale specific intention: "By Your Spirit, I will speak truth in love." This breath-synchronized commitment recognizes dependence on the divine breath (Pneuma) for lasting change.

This practice embodies the spiritual reality that the same divine breath that convicts of sin also carries forgiveness and empowerment. As Jesus breathes on His disciples and says, **"Receive the Holy Spirit. If you forgive anyone's sins, their sins are forgiven" (John 20:22-23)**, your breath becomes a tangible connection to this spiritual authority over sin.

## Divine Image Restoration Meditation

Many spiritual wounds involve distorted perceptions of God and self. Scripture affirms that we are created in God's image (Genesis 1:27) and that beholding Christ transforms us into His likeness (2 Corinthians 3:18). This meditation facilitates this restoration through breath-centered contemplation.

**Breath-Enhanced Practice**: Sit comfortably with eyes closed and:

CHAPTER TWELVE:
Meditation for Healing
And Restoration

1. **False Image Release**: Identify distorted images of God. You may have absorbed God as a harsh judge, a distant observer, a demanding taskmaster, or a cosmic killjoy. With each exhalation, release these false images: "Lord, you are not a harsh judge; that image is not You."

2. **True Image Reception**: Turn to Scripture's revelation of God's true nature. With each inhalation, receive a biblical truth about God: **"You are a compassionate Father" (based on Luke 15:20)**. With each exhalation, allow this truth to replace the false image.

3. **Self-Image Alignment**: As your image of God transforms, allow your self-image to align with how God sees you. Inhale the truth of your identity in Christ; exhale false identities based on performance, comparison, or condemnation.

4. **Transformative Beholding**: Conclude with several minutes of breath-centered contemplation of Christ. With each breath cycle, focus on an aspect of His character revealed in the Gospels. This "beholding" activates the transformative process described in 2 Corinthians 3:18, facilitated by the divine breath (Pneuma).

This practice recognizes that spiritual healing often requires addressing root perceptions of God and self. The divine breath serves as both the revealer of false images and the carrier of truth that restores the divine image within you, fulfilling God's original design established at creation.

## Spiritual Authority Breathing

Some spiritual wounds result from demonic oppression or spiritual warfare. Scripture affirms believers' authority in Christ: "The one who is in you is greater than the one who is in the world" (1 John 4:4). This meditation activates this spiritual authority through breath awareness.

**Breath-Enhanced Practice**: Go ahead and Stand in a posture of confidence (if physically able) and:

1. **Identity Affirmation**: Begin with deep breathing while affirming your position in Christ. With each inhalation, receive the truth: **"I am seated with Christ in heavenly places"** (based on Ephesians 2:6). With each exhalation, release any sense of spiritual defeat or victimhood.

2. **Authority Recognition**: Continue breathing deeply while recognizing the authority delegated to you in Christ. Inhale the truth: **"All authority in heaven and earth belongs to Jesus" (Matthew 28:18)**. Exhale the acknowledgment: **"And I am His ambassador" (2 Corinthians 5:20).**

3. **Resistance Declaration**: Use your breath to empower declarations against spiritual oppression. Inhale God's strength; exhale authoritative commands: **"In Jesus' name, I resist fear."** This breath-empowered resistance fulfills James 4:7: "Resist the devil, and he will flee from you."

4. **Kingdom Alignment**: Conclude by aligning with God's kingdom purposes. Inhale God's reign; exhale your surrender to His purposes: **"Your kingdom come,**

**Your will be done**" (Matthew 6:10). This breath centered alignment acknowledges that spiritual authority functions properly only within submission to God's ultimate authority.

This practice recognizes the connection between the divine breath and spiritual authority. When Jesus conferred authority on His disciples, He **"breathed on them and said, 'Receive the Holy Spirit'" (John 20:22)**. Your conscious breathing reminds you of this Spirit-empowered authority that displaces spiritual oppression with the reign of God.

# Integrating Healing into Daily Life

While dedicated meditation sessions facilitate healing, true restoration requires integration into daily life. Scripture emphasizes this ongoing nature of healing: **"Therefore we do not lose heart. Though outwardly we are wasting away, yet inwardly we are being renewed day by day." 2 Corinthians 4:16 (NIV)**

These practices help extend meditation's healing benefits beyond formal sessions.

### Breath Reminders Throughout the Day

Regular breath awareness is a practical means of maintaining a connection with God's healing presence throughout daily activities. Jesus modeled this continuous communion with the Father even amid busy ministries.

**Breath-Enhanced Practice**: Establish regular breath reminders in your daily routine:

1. **Scheduled Pauses**: Set reminders (phone alerts, specific activities, or time intervals) to pause for three conscious breaths, reconnecting with the divine breath (Ruach) that sustains and heals you.

2. **Transition Breathing**: Use transitions between activities to heal breath awareness. Before entering a meeting, starting your car, or beginning a meal, take three deep breaths while silently praying, "Lord, your healing presence goes with me."

3. **Response Breathing**: When symptoms, pain, or emotional triggers arise, immediately turn to conscious breathing as a first response. Inhale God's presence; exhale the symptom or reaction. This doesn't deny reality, but places it immediately in God's healing context.

4. **Gratitude Breathing**: Regularly pause for breath-centered gratitude for healing already received. This fulfills the biblical pattern of acknowledging God's work: **"Praise the LORD, my soul, and forget not all his benefits—who... heals all your diseases." Psalm 103:2-3 (NIV)**

These breath reminders transform ordinary moments into healing opportunities, fulfilling Paul's instruction to "pray continually" (1 Thessalonians 5:17). The divine breath becomes a constant companion in your healing journey, available in every circumstance and location.

## Community Support for Healing

Scripture emphasizes that healing often occurs in community: **"Confess your sins to each other and pray for each other**

**so that you may be healed" (James 5:16)**. While personal meditation is valuable, shared practices can amplify healing effects.

**Breath-Enhanced Practice**: Engage a healing-focused community through:

1. **Prayer Partnerships**: Establish regular prayer meetings with trusted believers where breath awareness is incorporated into intercession. As you pray for each other's healing, breathe deeply together, recognizing that the same divine breath (Pneuma) dwells in each believer.

2. **Group Meditation**: Participate in or initiate group meditation gatherings focused on healing. The synchronized breathing of believers creates a powerful environment for God's healing presence, fulfilling Jesus's promise: **"Where two or three gather in my name, there am I with them" (Matthew 18:20)**.

3. **Accountability Relationships**: Share your healing journey with trusted friends who can provide encouragement, perspective, and accountability for maintaining healing practices. Regular check-ins about breath-centered meditation help sustain commitment.

4. **Service Orientation**: As you experience healing, use breath-centered practices while serving others in their healing journeys. This fulfills the biblical pattern that we comfort others with the comfort we ourselves have received (2 Corinthians 1:4).

These community practices recognize that while healing is personal, it's not meant to be private. The divine breath flows within individuals and among the community of believers, creating a shared atmosphere where healing flourishes.

## Patience with the Healing Process

Scripture reves that healing often unfolds as a process rather than an instantaneous event. Jesus sometimes healed progressively (Mark 8:22-26), and Paul acknowledged the "not yet" aspect of our complete restoration (Romans 8:23-25). Meditation helps develop patience with this process.

**Breath-Enhanced Practice**: When healing seems slow or incomplete

1. **Present Moment Awareness**: Use your breath to anchor yourself in the present moment rather than fixating on future outcomes. With each inhalation, receive God's presence in this moment, and with each exhalation, release anxiety about the pace or completeness of healing.

2. **Progress Recognition**: Regularly pause for breath-centered reflection on healing progress already experienced. Inhale gratitude; exhale discouragement about what remains unhealed. This balanced perspective prevents all-or-nothing thinking about healing.

3. **Divine Timing Acceptance**: When impatience arises, use breath to surrender to God's timing. Inhale the truth: **"He has made everything beautiful in its time" (Ecclesiastes 3:11)**; exhale demands immediate results.

4. **Hope Cultivation**: Use breath to anchor hope when healing seems distant. Inhale the promise: **"I will**

**restore you to health and heal your wounds"
(Jeremiah 30:17);** exhale despair and resignation. This breath-anchored hope sustains you through the healing journey.

This practice acknowledges that the divine breath works in divine timing. Just as God hovered his breath over creation for six days before establishing rest, God's perfect wisdom may unfold your healing in stages. Each breath becomes not just a plea for healing but an act of trust in the Healer's perfect timing.

# Conclusion: The Continuous Healing Breath

As we conclude our exploration of meditation for healing and restoration, remember that the breath of life flowing through you right now is not merely biological respiration, but a continuous connection to the God who heals. Each breath you take carries the potential for divine restoration—physical, emotional, or spiritual.

The Hebrew understanding of Neshama and the Greek concept of Pneuma both reveal that God has designed your breathing as a channel for His healing presence. This isn't mystical imagination but biblical reality—the same divine breath that first animated humanity continues to restore, renew, and transform those who cultivate receptivity through meditation.

As you develop your meditation practice, let each conscious breath remind you of God's promise: **"I am the LORD, who**

**heals you" (Exodus 15:26).** The divine breath within you is not passive but actively working, not distant but intimately present, not limited, but continuously available to bring healing to every dimension of your being.

In the next chapter, we'll explore how meditation facilitates transformation—the progressive journey of becoming more like Christ through renewing your mind, heart, and life. This transformative dimension complements the healing aspect of meditation, as restoration leads naturally to growth and maturity in Christ.

# CHAPTER THIRTEEN:
# Meditation for Transformation

The ultimate purpose of Christian meditation is not merely information acquisition, emotional comfort, or even spiritual experiences, but transformation into the likeness of Christ. As Paul writes, **"And we all, who with unveiled faces contemplate the Lord's glory, are being transformed into his image with ever-increasing glory, which comes from the Lord, who is the Spirit." 2 Cor. 3:18 (NIV)**

This transformation represents the fulfillment of God's eternal purpose: **"For those God foreknew he also predestined to be conformed to the image of his Son." Rom. 8:29 (NIV)**

This chapter will explore how meditation facilitates this transformative process, moving beyond techniques to the profound inner change God desires to work in every believer.

## Divine Breath as Agent of Transformation

Before examining specific meditation practices, it's essential to understand how the breath of life serves as a divine agent of transformation. The connection between breath and transformation appears throughout Scripture, revealing God's design for your spiritual development.

In **Genesis 2:7**, God formed Adam from dust and **"breathed into his nostrils the breath of life." This divine breath (Neshama)** didn't merely animate a physical body but transformed dust into a living being bearing God's image. Similarly, your spiritual transformation isn't simply behavioral metafiction, but a truly profound re-creation empowered by the same divine breath.

This transformative power of the divine breath appears again in Ezekiel's vision of dry bones. God commands, **"I will put breath in you, and you will come to life" (Ezek. 37:6**). As the breath enters, the bones not only live but are transformed into "a vast army" (Ezek. 37:10)—a complete metamorphosis from death to vibrant life. This prophetic image reveals how the divine breath transforms individual believers and the entire faith community.

In the New Testament, this transformative breath reaches its fullest expression when Jesus **"breathed on them and said, 'Receive the Holy Spirit'" (John 20:22).** This divine breath (*pneuma*) transformed fearful disciples hiding behind locked doors into bold witnesses empowered for mission. The same transformative breath dwells within you now, making your breathing a sacred connection to the Spirit who transforms you into Christ's image.

The Hebrew letters of **_ruach_ (רוּחַ)** reveal this transformative dimension: the **Resh (ר)** representing God's holiness that transforms your character, the **Vav (ו)** connecting heaven and earth to transform your perspective, and the **Cheth (ח)** binding you to God in a covenant relationship where transformation flourishes. With each conscious breath, you engage this divine transformative presence—drawing in God's holiness, connecting spiritual reality with earthly existence, and strengthening the covenant bond where transformation occurs.

As you approach meditation for transformation, recognize that your breath isn't merely a focusing technique but a tangible connection to the divine Transformer. Each breath carries the potential for profound change as you inhale God's transforming presence and exhale resistance to His work. This understanding transforms meditation from a self-improvement strategy into a genuine surrender to the Spirit, who **"transforms us into his image with ever-increasing glory" (2 Corinthians 3:18)**.

# Understanding Biblical Transformation

Before examining specific meditation practices, it's essential to understand what Scripture means by transformation and how it differs from other types of change.

## Transformation vs. Modification

Many approaches to personal change focus on behavior modification—altering external actions through willpower, habit formation, or environmental adjustments. While these approaches may produce visible results, they often leave the inner person unchanged. Jesus criticized this superficial change in the Pharisees: **"You clean the outside of the cup and dish, but inside they are full of greed and self-indulgence" (Matt. 23:25)**.

Biblical transformation works from the inside out. The Greek word for "transformed" in Romans 12:2 is *metamorphoō*, from which we get "metamorphosis"—a complete change of form, as when a caterpillar becomes a butterfly. This transformation isn't merely adjusting behaviors, but becoming a new creation with a different nature.

This inside-out transformation parallels how the divine breath operates. In creation, God first breathed life into Adam's innermost being, and that internal transformation naturally produced external results. Similarly, the Holy Spirit (*pneuma*) works first on your inner nature, and changed behavior flows naturally from this renewed core. Your conscious breathing during meditation is a physical reminder of this inside-out transformative process.

## The Process of Transformation

Scripture reveals several key aspects of how transformation occurs:

### 1. Divine Initiative and Human Response

Transformation begins with God's initiative: **"For it is God who works in you to will and to act to fulfill his good purpose" (Phil. 2:13)**. Yet it also requires human cooperation: **"Continue to work out your salvation with fear and trembling" (Phil. 2:12).** This paradoxical partnership means transformation is neither passive reception nor self-generated effort, but active cooperation with divine grace.

The breath itself beautifully illustrates this partnership. Each breath involves both receiving (inhaling) and responding

[218]

(exhaling)—you cannot do one without the other. Similarly, transformation involves receiving and actively responding to God's transforming grace. Your conscious breathing during meditation embodies this divine-human partnership, as each breath cycle represents receiving God's initiative and offering your response.

## 2. Mind Renewal as the Gateway

**Romans 12:2** identifies mind renewal as the pathway to transformation: **"Do not conform to the pattern of this world but be transformed by the renewing of your mind."** The mind, including thoughts, beliefs, values, and perceptions, serves as the gateway for transformation. As thinking changes, being changes.

The divine breath plays a crucial role in this mind renewal. In Hebrew thought, the mind isn't separate from the spirit (*ruach*) but an expression of it. When you engage in breath-centered meditation, you're not merely calming mental activity but inviting the divine *Ruach* to renew your mind from within. Each conscious breath becomes an opportunity for the Spirit to **"take captive every thought to make it obedient to Christ" (2 Cor. 10:5).**

## 3. Progressive Rather Than Instantaneous

While conversion may occur momentarily, transformation unfolds progressively. Paul describes this process as moving **"from glory to glory"** (2 Cor. 3:18 NKJV) or with **"ever-increasing glory"** (NIV). This progressive nature explains why even mature believers continue experiencing a more profound transformation.

[219]

This progressive transformation reflects the rhythm of breathing. Each breath builds upon previous breaths in a continuous flow, just as spiritual transformation unfolds breath by breath, moment by moment, day by day. Your conscious breathing during meditation acknowledges this progressive nature, recognizing that transformation comes not through occasional dramatic experiences but through consistent engagement with the divine breath that gradually reshapes your being.

## 4. Suffering as Catalyst

Scripture frequently connects transformation with suffering: **"And the God of all grace, who called you to his eternal glory in Christ, after you have suffered a little while, will himself restore you and make you strong, firm and steadfast"(1 Pet. 5:10)**. These difficulties often speed up transformation by revealing areas needing change and creating openness to God's work.

The breath offers wisdom for navigating suffering's transformative potential. When physical or emotional pain arises, your natural tendency is to hold your breath or breathe shallowly, resisting the experience as it arises. Yet true transformation comes through breathing deep into the suffering—neither denying it nor being overwhelmed by it, but allowing the divine breath to flow through it. This breath centered approach to suffering fulfills Paul's desire to **"know Christ... and the fellowship of sharing in his sufferings, becoming like him in his death" (Phil. 3:10)**.

## 5. Community as Context

While transformation involves individual experience, it occurs optimally within a community. Paul writes that when each part of the body of Christ works appropriately, it **"builds itself up in love" (Eph. 4:16)**. The interactions, accountability, and support of authentic Christian community provide an essential context for transformation.

This communal dimension reflects the nature of breath itself. The air you breathe is shared—the same air circulates among all living beings. Similarly, all believers share the divine breath (Pneuma), creating a spiritual ecosystem where individual transformation contributes to collective transformation. Your conscious breathing during community meditation acknowledges this shared reality, as the same Spirit breathes through each person, creating unity amid diversity.

Understanding these aspects of biblical transformation helps us approach meditation not as a technique for self-improvement, but to cooperate with God's transformative work. Meditation creates the conditions for transformation by bringing us into sustained, attentive contact with God's truth and presence through the divine breath.

# The Role of Meditation in Transformation

Christian meditation contributes to transformation through several specific breath-centered mechanisms:

## 1. Extended Exposure to Truth

Transformation requires more than brief exposure to truth; it demands prolonged engagement that allows truth to penetrate beyond intellectual understanding to heart-level conviction. As **Psalm 1:2** describes the blessed person: **"but whose delight is in the law of the LORD, and who meditates on his Law Day and night**."

**Breath-Enhanced Application**: During meditation, your breath serves as a vehicle for truth absorption. As you inhale, imagine drawing Scripture deeper into your being; as you exhale, allow it to permeate your thoughts, emotions, and will. This breath-synchronized engagement with truth fulfills **Jeremiah 15:16: "When your words came, I ate them; they were my joy and my heart's delight."**

The divine breath (*ruach*) that inspired Scripture now dwells within you, creating a profound resonance between the written word and the indwelling Spirit. Your conscious breathing during Scripture meditation activates this resonance, allowing the truth to transform you from within.

## 2. Heightened Receptivity to the Spirit

Transformation is ultimately the work of the Holy Spirit, who applies Christ's finished work to our lives. Meditation creates receptivity to this divine work by quieting competing voices and making space for the Spirit's gentle influence. As Jesus promises, **"When he, the Spirit of truth, comes, he will guide you into all the truth" (John 16:13).**

**Breath-Enhanced Application**: The biblical connection between breath and Spirit (both *ruach* and *pneuma* mean "breath" and "spirit") reveals that your breathing can become a tangible point of connection with the Holy Spirit. As you breathe consciously during meditation, silently acknowledge: "This breath connects me to Your Spirit." This breath-awareness creates heightened receptivity to the Spirit's transforming work.

This isn't merely symbolic but reflects the spiritual reality that the same divine breath that hovered over creation now dwells within you, continuously working to form Christ's image in your life. Your conscious breathing acknowledges and engages in His indwelling presence.

## 3. Integration of Head and Heart

Transformation requires truth from intellectual understanding to heart-level conviction that shapes desires, choices, and actions. Meditation facilitates this integration by engaging in the rational and affective dimensions of our being. **Proverbs 23:7** suggests, **"As he thinks in his heart, so is he,"** highlighting the connection between deep thoughts and identity.

**Breath-Enhanced Application**: Your breath naturally bridges mind, heart, thought, and emotion. During meditation, use your breath to integrate intellectual understanding with emotional resonance: Inhale a biblical truth; exhale its personal application. Inhale God's perspective; exhale your emotional response. This breath-centered integration fulfills the greatest commandment to love God with all your heart, soul, mind, and strength (Mark 12:30)—your entire being unified in response to God.

The divine breath (*neshama*) that initially integrated your physical, mental, emotional, and spiritual dimensions continues this integrative work through conscious breathing, restoring the wholeness that sin has fragmented.

## 4. Sustained Attention to God's Presence

Transformation occurs through beholding Christ: **"And we all, who with unveiled faces contemplate the Lord's glory, are being transformed into his image with ever-increasing glory, which comes from the Lord, who is the Spirit." 2 Cor. 3:18 (NIV)** Meditation trains the capacity for this contemplative beholding, developing sustained attention to God's presence that allows His transforming influence to penetrate deeply.

**Breath-Enhanced Application**: Your breath is an anchor for attention during contemplative meditation. When distractions arise, gently focus on your breathing as a tangible connection to God's presence. With each inhalation, receive God's presence, and with each exhalation, release distractions. This breath-anchored attention fulfills David's aspiration: **"One thing I ask from the LORD, this only do I seek: that I may dwell in the house of the LORD all the days of my life, to gaze on the beauty of the LORD and to seek him in his temple." Psalm 27:4 (NIV).**

The divine breath within you creates a portable sanctuary— wherever you are, your breathing can become a point of connection with God's transforming presence. This fulfills the New Testament revelation that your body is the temple of the Holy Spirit (1 Cor. 6:19), with each breath providing an opportunity for sanctuary awareness.

## 5. Embodied Practice of Surrender

Transformation requires surrender to God's work— releasing control and yielding to divine initiative. Meditation provides a concrete, embodied practice of this surrender through the deliberate setting aside of personal agendas to receive God's presence and truth. As Jesus modeled, **"Not my will, but yours be done" (Luke 22:42).**

**Breath-Enhanced Application**: Your breathing offers the practice of complete surrender. With each exhalation, you consciously release something you've been controlling or clinging to; with each inhalation, receive God's governance in that area. This breath-synchronized surrender acknowledges that true transformation comes not through self-effort, but through yielding to the divine breath that transforms from within.

This practice embodies Jesus's teaching that **"whoever wants to save their life will lose it, but whoever loses their life for me will find it" (Matt. 16:25)**. Each breath becomes a mini death to self and reception of God's life, fulfilling Paul's testimony: **"I have been crucified with Christ and I no longer live, but Christ lives in me" (Gal. 2:20).**

By engaging these breath-enhanced mechanisms during meditation, you create optimal conditions for the Holy Spirit's transformative work. Your breathing becomes not just a focusing technique but a sacred participation in the divine process of being **"transformed into his image with ever-increasing glory" (2 Cor. 3:18).**

# Meditation Practices for Character Transformation

Character transformation—the development of Christ-like virtues and the diminishment of sinful tendencies—stands at the heart of the Christian journey. Paul describes this process as putting off the old self and putting on the new self (Eph. 4:22-24). Meditation facilitates this transformation by focusing on specific character qualities and creating space for the Spirit's formative work.

## Fruit of the Spirit Meditation

In Galatians 5:22-23, Paul identifies nine qualities the Holy Spirit produces in believers: love, joy, peace, patience, kindness, goodness, faithfulness, gentleness, and self-control. We don't achieve these qualities through human effort; instead, we cultivate them by cooperating with the Spirit's work.

**Breath-Enhanced Practice**: Select one fruit of the Spirit to focus on during meditation. Then:

1. **Scriptural Grounding**: Read passages that reveal this quality in God's character and Christ's life. For

example, if focusing on patience, read about God's patience in 2 Peter 3:9 and Christ's patience in 1 Timothy 1:16.

2. **Breath-Centered Reflection**: Close your eyes and establish a deep, conscious breathing rhythm. With each inhalation, receive this divine quality: **"Lord, I breathe in Your patience."** Release the opposing quality with each exhalation: **"I breathe out my impatience and hurry."**

3. **Imaginative Engagement**: As you continue breathing, imagine specific situations where this fruit is needed. With each breath cycle, envision responding with this Spirit-produced quality rather than your natural tendency.

4. **Prayerful Surrender**: Conclude by acknowledging your dependence on the Spirit for producing this fruit. With each inhalation, express receptivity: **"Spirit, produce Your patience in me."** With each exhalation, release self-effort: **"I cannot generate this through my strength."**

This practice acknowledges that character transformation comes "not by might nor by power, but by my Spirit, says the LORD Almighty" (Zechariah 4:6). Your breathing becomes a tangible connection to this Spirit, who produces Christ-like character from within.

## Virtue Formation Meditation

Beyond the fruit of the Spirit, Scripture calls believers to cultivate virtues that reflect Christ's character. Peter encourages adding to faith **goodness, knowledge, self-control, perseverance, godliness, mutual affection, and love (2 Peter 1:5-7)**. Meditation helps develop these virtues through focused attention and divine partnership. Breath-Enhanced Practice: Select a specific virtue to develop. Then:

1. **Definition Clarity**: Begin by clearly defining this virtue from Scripture. For example, if focusing on courage, examine how Joshua was commanded to "be strong and courageous" (Joshua 1:9) and how this virtue manifests in biblical examples.

2. **Breath-Synchronized Affirmation**: Establish a rhythm of deep breathing while affirming this virtue's presence in your life through Christ. Inhale: "Through Christ" — Exhale: "I am becoming courageous." This breath-carried affirmation acknowledges both the divine source and the progressive development of virtue.

3. **Obstacle Identification**: As you continue breathing deeply, identify internal obstacles to this virtue— fears, false beliefs, or habits that hinder its expression. With each exhalation, release these obstacles: "I release my fear of rejection."

4. **Practical Application**: Conclude by identifying specific situations where you can practice this virtue. With each breath cycle, commit to concrete expression: Inhale God's empowerment; exhale

particular action: "I will speak truth lovingly in tomorrow's meeting."

This practice embodies Peter's instruction to "make every effort to add to your faith these virtues (2 Peter 1:5) while recognizing that this effort involves cooperation with the divine breath rather than mere self-improvement. Your breathing becomes a physical reminder of this cooperative process of virtue formation.

## Besetting Sin Transformation

While focusing primarily on positive virtue development, Christian growth also involves addressing sinful patterns that hinder Christ-likeness. Paul instructs believers to "put to death whatever belongs to your earthly nature" (Colossians 3:5). Meditation helps identify and transform these patterns through the power of the Spirit.

**Breath-Enhanced Practice**: Identify a specific sin pattern to address. Then:

1. **Honest Acknowledgment**: Begin with breath-centered confession, acknowledging this sin pattern without minimization or excuse. Inhale God's holiness; exhale honest confession: "Lord, I confess my persistent anger."

2. **Root Cause Discernment**: As you continue breathing deeply, invite the Holy Spirit to reveal root causes of this pattern—unmet needs, false beliefs, or wounds that drive the behavior. Inhale divine insight; exhale self-deception: "Show me what drives this pattern."

3. **Gospel Application**: Focus your breathing on receiving the specific aspect of Christ's finished work

that addresses this sin. Inhale the truth: **"In Christ, I died to anger's pow**er" (based on Romans 6:6-7); exhale the lie: **"I must control others through anger."**

4.  **Replacement Virtue**: Conclude by breathing in the positive virtue that replaces this sin pattern. Inhale**: "I receive Christ's gentleness"**; exhale: **"I release my right to anger."** This fulfills Paul's teaching to **"put off the old self... and put on the new self" (Ephesians 4:22-24).**

This practice recognizes that freedom from sin comes not through willpower but through the transforming power of the divine breath (Pneuma). As Paul writes, **"If by the Spirit you put to death the misdeeds of the body, you will live" (Romans 8:13)**, and as Jesus taught, **"No branch can bear fruit by itself; it must remain in the vine" (John 15:4**). Your conscious breathing becomes a tangible connection to this Spirit-empowered mortification of sin.

# Meditation Practices for Mind Transformation

Since Romans 12:2 identifies mind renewal as the pathway to transformation, specific meditation practices that address thought patterns are essential. These practices help fulfill Paul's instruction to **"take captive every thought to make it obedient to Christ" (2 Cor. 10:5).**

## Truth-Centered Thought Meditation

Many destructive behaviors and emotions stem from false beliefs—distortions about God, self, others, or reality that contradict Scripture. Meditation helps identify and transform these beliefs through sustained focus on biblical truth.

**Breath-Enhanced Practice**: Identify a specific false belief influencing your life. Then:

1. **Belief Identification**: Begin by clearly articulating this belief: "I believe I must be perfect to be accepted." Breathe deeply as you acknowledge how this belief has shaped your thoughts, feelings, and actions.

2. **Truth Discovery**: Search Scripture for specific truths that counter this false belief. For example, for perfectionism, Ephesians 1:6 reveals acceptance in Christ regardless of performance.

3. **Breath-Synchronized Replacement**: Establish a rhythm of deep breathing while replacing false beliefs with biblical truths. Inhale: "In Christ" — Exhale: "I am already fully accepted." Allow the divine breath to carry this truth deep into your consciousness.

4. **Practical Reframing**: As you breathe, identify specific situations where this truth applies. With each breath cycle, reframe your understanding: Inhale God's perspective; exhale your distorted view. This breath-centered reframing fulfills the renewing of your mind" (Rom to transform the instruction. 12:2).

This practice acknowledges that the divine breath (*ruach*) that inspired Scripture now dwells within you, empowering the internalization of truth. Your conscious breathing becomes a vehicle for this truth to move from intellectual assent to heart-level conviction that transforms your entire being.

## Thought Pattern Awareness Meditation

Beyond specific beliefs, Scripture calls attention to broader thought patterns that shape character and behavior. Paul instructs believers to think about whatever is true, noble, correct, pure, lovely, admirable, excellent, and praiseworthy (Phil. 4:8). Meditation helps develop awareness and intentionality regarding these thought patterns.

**Breath-Enhanced Practice**: This practice develops awareness of thought patterns through breath-centered observation:

1. **Centering**: Begin with several minutes of deep, conscious breathing, establishing a state of alert receptivity.

2. **Observation**: As you continue breathing steadily, observe the thoughts that naturally arise without judging or engaging them. Notice patterns, themes, and emotional tones in your thinking.

3. **Evaluation**: With each breath cycle, evaluate observed thoughts against Philippians 4:8 criteria. Inhale discernment; exhale judgment: "Is this thought true? Is it beneficial?"

4. **Redirection**: When noticing unhelpful thought patterns, use your breath as a reset mechanism.

Inhale God's perspective; exhale the unproductive pattern. Consciously direct your attention to thoughts aligned with Philippians 4:8, allowing your breath to anchor this redirection.

This practice develops what early Christian writers called "watchfulness" (*nepsis*)—the ability to observe thoughts before fully identifying with them. The divine breath provides the space for this observation and the power for redirection, fulfilling Paul's instruction to **"take captive every thought to make it obedient to Christ" (2 Cor. 10:5).**

## Identity Renewal Meditation

Many thought patterns stem from identity confusion—forgetting or disbelieving who we are in Christ. Scripture emphasizes the importance of knowing and living from our true identity: **"See what great love the Father has lavished on us, that we should be called children of God! And that is what we are!" 1 John 3:1 (NIV)** Meditation helps establish this identity as the foundation for transformed thinking.

**Breath-Enhanced Practice**: This practice reinforces true identity through breath-centered affirmation:

1. **Identity Scripture Selection**: Begin by selecting passages that reveal your identity in Christ, such as Ephesians 1:3-14, Romans 8:14-17, or 1 Peter 2:9-10.

2. **Breath-Synchronized Affirmation**: Read these passages slowly, then close your eyes and establish a

[233]

rhythm of deep breathing. With each inhalation, receive a specific aspect of your identity: **"I am God's chosen child."** With each exhalation, release false identities: **"My performance does not define me."**

3.  **Embodied Awareness**: As you breathe, notice how different identity statements affect your body, emotions, and thoughts. Allow the divine breath to carry these truths into your mind and physical being.

4.  **Lived Expression**: Conclude by identifying how this identity shapes daily life. With each breath cycle, connect identity to action: Inhale: **"As God's beloved child"** — Exhale: **"I live with confidence and compassion."**

This practice implements Paul's teaching about "putting off the old self... and putting on the new self, created to be like God in true righteousness and holiness" (Eph. 4:22-24). The divine breath serves as both the reminder of your true identity established at creation and the empowerment to live from that identity daily.

# Meditation Practices for Heart Transformation

While mind renewal provides the gateway to transformation, lasting change must reach the heart—the core of desires, values, and motivations. Jesus emphasized this heart transformation: **"For where your treasure is, there your**

**heart will be also" (Matt. 6:21).** Meditation helps align the heart with God's values and desires.

## Desire Reordering Meditation

Scripture acknowledges the power of desires in shaping behavior and calls for their reordering according to God's priorities. As David prayed, **"Delight yourself in the LORD, and he will give you the desires of your heart" (Ps. 37:4).** Meditation helps identify and reorder desires through sustained attention to God's beauty and goodness.

**Breath-Enhanced Practice**: This practice addresses desire reordering through breath-centered awareness:

1. **Desire Identification**: Begin with deep breathing while prayerfully asking, "What do I most deeply want?" Allow desires to surface without judgment, noticing their intensity and influence.

2. **Divine Desire Invitation**: Continue breathing deeply while inviting God to shape your desires. Inhale: "Lord, shape my wanting"; exhale: "according to Your will." This breath-synchronized prayer acknowledges that desire transformation comes through divine initiative rather than mere willpower.

3. **Scripture Saturation**: Meditate on passages that reveal God's desires, such as Micah 6:8 or Philippians 2:1-11. With each inhalation, receive God's desires; with each exhalation, release competing desires. Allow the divine breath to align your wanting with God's gradually.

4.  **Practical Redirection**: Conclude by identifying specific ways to nurture godly desires and starve unhealthy ones. With each breath cycle, commit to concrete practices: Inhale commitment to what feeds godly desire; exhale what inflames competing desires.

This practice recognizes that desire transformation occurs not through suppression but through the cultivation of greater desires. The divine breath (*ruach*) that first animated human desire now works to restore its proper orientation toward God and His purposes, fulfilling Augustine's insight that our hearts are restless until they rest in God.

## Emotional Healing Meditation

Emotional wounds and patterns often drive behavior in ways that hinder Christ-likeness. Scripture acknowledges these emotional realities while pointing to healing: **"He heals the brokenhearted and binds up their wounds" (Ps. 147:3)**. Meditation creates space for this emotional healing as part of heart transformation.

**Breath-Enhanced Practice**: This practice addresses emotional healing through breath-centered awareness:

1.  **Emotional Awareness**: Begin with slow, deep breathing while asking, "What am I feeling right now?" Allow emotions to surface without judgment or suppression, noticing their presence in your body.

2.  **Compassionate Presence**: Continue breathing while extending compassion toward these painful emotions. Inhale God's compassion; exhale self-

judgment about feelings. This breath-centered compassion acknowledges that emotions aren't sinful but provide important information.

3. **Divine Companionship**: Invite God's presence into each emotion, especially those that feel overwhelming or unacceptable. With each inhalation, receive God's presence in this feeling; with each exhalation, release isolation in the emotion. This breath-synchronized invitation fulfills the promise that God is "close to the brokenhearted" (Ps. 34:18).

4. **Emotional Integration**: Conclude by integrating emotions into your spiritual journey rather than compartmentalizing them. With each breath cycle, acknowledge how even difficult emotions can serve transformation when brought into God's presence.

This practice recognizes that the divine breath (*neshama*) that first integrated your emotional capacity works to heal and restore it. Your conscious breathing becomes a tangible connection to this healing presence, allowing emotions to be transformed rather than merely managed or suppressed.

## Value Alignment Meditation

Our values—what we consider most important and worthy—drive countless daily decisions and shape our character over time. Jesus emphasized value alignment: **"For where your treasure is, there your heart will be also" (Matt. 6:21).** Meditation helps identify and align values with God's kingdom priorities.

# CHAPTER THIRTEEN:
## Meditation for Transformation

**Breath-Enhanced Practice**: This practice addresses value alignment through breath-centered reflection:

1. **Value Identification**: Begin with deep breathing while reflecting on your value, as revealed by how you spend time, money, attention, and energy. Notice any gaps between stated values and lived values.

2. **Kingdom Value Exploration**: Study Jesus's teachings about kingdom values, particularly in the Sermon on the Mount (Matthew 5-7). Each inhalation receives a specific kingdom value; with each exhalation, competing cultural values are released.

3. **Value Realignment**: Continue breathing deeply while consciously realigning your values with God's. Inhale: **"Lord, I value what You value"**; exhale: **"I release what the world values."** This breath-synchronized realignment fulfills Jesus's instruction to **"seek first his kingdom and righteousness" (Matthew 6:33).**

4. **Practical Expression**: Conclude by identifying decisions to express this value realignment. With each breath cycle, commit to concrete choices: inhale commitment to kingdom values; exhale worldly value systems.

This practice recognizes that value transformation occurs not through mere intellectual assent, but through heart-level reorientation. The divine breath is both the revealer of actual value and the empowerment to live according to kingdom priorities, fulfilling Paul's instruction: **"Set your minds on things above, not on earthly things" (Colossians 3:2).**

# Integrating Transformation into Daily Life.

While dedicated meditation sessions facilitate transformation, lasting change requires integration into daily life. Paul emphasizes this ongoing nature of transformation: **"And we all... are being transformed into his image with ever-increasing glory" (2 Corinthians 3:18).** These practices help extend meditation's transformative effects beyond formal sessions.

## Breath Reminders Throughout the Day

Regular breath awareness is a practical means of maintaining transformative consciousness amid daily activities. Jesus modeled this continuous communion with the Father even amid busy ministries.

**Breath-Enhanced Practice**: Establish regular breath reminders in your daily routine:

1. **Scheduled Pauses**: Set reminders (phone alerts, specific activities, or time intervals) to pause for three conscious breaths, reconnecting with the transformative presence of the divine breath (Ruach).

2. **Transition Breathing**: Use transitions between activities as opportunities for transformative breath awareness. Before entering a meeting, starting your car, or beginning a meal, take three deep breaths while silently praying, "Lord, transform me in this moment."

3. **Response Breathing**: When facing triggers for old patterns or challenges to new virtues, immediately

[239]

turn to conscious breathing as a first response. Inhale, God's transforming presence exhale the old pattern. This breath-centered response creates space for transformed choices.

4. **Gratitude Breathing**: At regular intervals, pause for breath-centered gratitude for transformation already experienced. This fulfills Paul's instruction to **"give thanks in all circumstances" (1 Thessalonians 5:18)** while reinforcing awareness of God's transforming work.

These breath reminders transform ordinary moments into transformation opportunities, fulfilling Paul's instruction to "pray continually" (1 Thessalonians 5:17). The divine breath becomes a constant companion in your transformation journey, available in every circumstance and location.

## Community Support for Transformation

Scripture emphasizes that transformation occurs optimally within the community: **"As iron sharpens iron, so one person sharpens another" (Proverbs 27:17)**. While personal meditation is valuable, shared practices can amplify transformative effects.

Breath-Enhanced Practice: Engage a transformation-focused community through:

1. **Accountability Partnerships: Establish regular meetings with trusted believers, incorporating breath awareness into accountability.** Begin these conversations with shared conscious breathing, recognizing that the same divine breath (Pneuma) dwells in each believer.

2. **Group Meditation**: take part in or initiate group meditation gatherings focused on transformation. The synchronized breathing of believers creates a powerful environment for God's transforming presence, fulfilling Jesus's promise: "Where two or three gather in my name, there am I with them" (Matthew 18:20).

3. **Transformative Feedback**: Invite trusted friends to provide feedback on your transformation journey, receiving this input with breath-centered humility. Inhale openness to truth; exhale defensiveness. This breath-synchronized receptivity fulfills **Proverbs 12:1: "Whoever loves discipline loves knowledge, but whoever hates correction is stupid."**

4. **Shared Celebration**: Regularly celebrate transformation observed in community members, using breath-centered gratitude to acknowledge God's work. This fulfills Paul's instruction to "rejoice with those who rejoice" (Romans 12:15) while reinforcing community awareness of God's amazing transforming presence.

These community practices recognize that while transformation is personal, it's not meant to be private. The divine breath flows within individuals and among the community of believers, creating a shared atmosphere where transformation flourishes.

## Patience with the Transformation Process

Scripture reveals that transformation unfolds progressively rather than instantaneously. Paul describes it as moving "from glory to glory" (2 Corinthians 3:18, NKJV) and acknowledges the tension between "already" and "not yet" in our experience. Meditation helps develop patience with this process.

**Breath-Enhanced Practice**: When transformation seems slow or incomplete:

1. **Present Moment Awareness**: Use your breath to anchor yourself in the present moment rather than fixating on future outcomes. With each inhalation, receive God's presence in this moment, and with each exhalation, release anxiety about the pace of transformation.

2. **Progress Recognition**: Regularly pause for breath-centered reflection on transformation already experienced. Inhale gratitude; exhale discouragement about what remains unchanged. This balanced perspective prevents all-or-nothing thinking about transformation.

3. **Divine Timing Acceptance**: When impatience arises, use breath to surrender to God's timing. Inhale the truth: "He who began a good work in you will carry it on to completion" (Philippians 1:6); exhale demands immediate results.

4. **Hope Cultivation**: Use breath to anchor hope when transformation seems distant. Inhale the promise: "We shall be like him, for we shall see him as he is" (1 John 3:2); exhale despair and resignation. This breath-anchored hope sustains you through the transformation journey.

This practice acknowledges that the divine breath works in divine timing. Just as a seed planted in the soil requires time to germinate and grow, the seeds of transformation planted through meditation require time to produce visible fruit. Each breath becomes not just a plea for transformation but an act of trust in the Transformer's perfect timing.

# Conclusion: The Continuous Transforming Breath

As we conclude our exploration of meditation for transformation, remember that the breath of life flowing through you right now is not merely biological respiration, but a continuous connection to the God who transforms. Each breath you take carries the potential for divine transformation—whether in character, mind, or heart.

The Hebrew understanding of Neshama and the Greek concept of Pneuma both reveal that God has designed your breathing as a channel for His transforming presence. This isn't mystical imagination but biblical reality—the same divine breath that first created humanity in God's image continues to restore that image in those who cultivate receptivity through meditation.

As you develop your meditation practice, let each conscious breath remind you of Paul's promise: "We all... are being transformed into his image with ever-increasing glory, which comes from the Lord, who is the Spirit" (2 Corinthians 3:18). The divine breath within you is not static but dynamic, not limited but continuously available to transform every dimension of your being into Christ's likeness.

In the next chapter, we'll explore establishing a sustainable, lifelong meditation practice supporting this ongoing trans-formation journey. We'll address practical considerations like consistency amid busy schedules, adaptation to different seasons of life, and integration with other spiritual disciplines.

CHAPTER FOURTEEN:
# Establishing A Sustainable Meditation Practice

While the previous chapters have explored Christian meditation's rich theological foundations and transformative potential, this chapter addresses a practical question: How do you establish a sustainable practice that endures beyond initial enthusiasm? As Jesus taught in the parable of the sower, spiritual beginnings don't guarantee lasting fruit. Some seeds spring up quickly but wither when challenges arise (Mark 4:5-6, 16-17). A sustainable meditation practice requires intentional cultivation to produce the **"crop, yielding a hundred, sixty or thirty times what was sown"** **(Matt. 13:23).**

## The Divine Breath as Sustaining Power

Before exploring practical strategies for sustainability, it's essential to understand how the breath of life serves as the divine sustaining power for your meditation practice. Scripture portrays God's breath as the initial source of life and the ongoing sustainer of all creation.

In **Job 33:4**, Elihu declares, **"The Spirit of God has made me; the breath of the Almighty gives me life."** The Hebrew reveals a profound truth: the divine breath (*neshama*) doesn't just create life once but continuously "gives" life—a present, ongoing action. Similarly, Psalm 104:29-30 shows that God's removal of His breath causes creatures to die, but His sending of His breath creates them and renews the ground. The divine breath's cyclical, sustaining nature provides the foundation for a sustainable meditation practice.

Jesus showed this sustaining power when He "breathed on them and said, 'Receive the Holy Spirit'" (John 20:22). This divine breath (*pneuma*) empowered the disciples not just for a momentary experience but for lifelong ministry. The same sustaining breath dwells within you now, making your breathing a sacred connection to the Spirit, who empowers consistent spiritual practice.

The Hebrew letters of **ruach** (רוּחַ) reveal this sustaining dimension: the **Resh (ר)** representing God's faithful presence that never abandons, the **Vav (ו)** connecting heaven's resources with earth's limitations, and the **Cheth (ח)** binding you to God in a covenant relationship where sustainability flourishes. With each conscious breath, you engage this divine sustaining presence—drawing in God's faithfulness, connecting infinite resources with finite capacity, and strengthening the covenant bond where consistency develops.

As you approach establishing a sustainable meditation practice, recognize that your breath isn't merely a technique for focus, but a tangible connection to the divine Sustainer.

Each breath carries the potential for renewed commitment as you inhale God's empowering presence and exhale self-reliance and discouragement. This understanding transforms meditation from a discipline maintained through willpower into a response to the Spirit who "helps us in our weakness" (Rom. 8:26) and sustains us through every challenge.

# Common Challenges to Sustainable Practice

Before developing sustainability strategies, it's helpful to identify common challenges that hinder consistent meditation practice. Scripture acknowledges these challenges while providing wisdom for addressing them.

## 1. Time Constraints

Perhaps the most frequently cited obstacle is a lack of time amid busy schedules. Jesus acknowledged this reality when He invited His disciples to **"come with me by yourselves to a quiet place and get some rest" (Mark 6:31)** amid ministry demands that left them without **"time to eat" (Mark 6:31).**

**Breath-Enhanced Response**: When time constraints threaten your practice, use your breath as a reminder of divine priorities. With each conscious breath, recall that the same God who sustains the universe through His breath has given you the time needed for what truly matters. Your breathing becomes a "selah" moment—a sacred pause that reorients priorities.

The divine breath (*ruach*) that ordered creation from chaos can similarly order your schedule according to divine wisdom. Each conscious breath becomes an opportunity to inhale God's perspective on time and exhale the tyranny of urgency that displaces spiritual priorities.

## 2. Mental Distractions

Internal distractions—wandering thoughts, persistent worries, and planning impulses—frequently disrupt meditation. Scripture acknowledges this challenge by describing the blessed person as one who successfully focuses on God's word despite competing mental activities (Psalms 1:2).

**Breath-Enhanced Response**: When distractions arise, use your breath as an anchor for returning attention. Rather than becoming frustrated with wandering thoughts, gently redirect focus to your breathing as a tangible connection to God's presence. This breath-centered refocusing acknowledges that distractions are normal while providing a consistent return point.

The divine breath (*neshama*) that first integrated your mental faculties continues this integrative work through conscious breathing, advancing the capacity for sustained attention. Each distraction becomes not a failure but an opportunity to practice the gentle return to presence through breath awareness.

## 3. Physical Restlessness

Physical discomfort, restlessness, or fatigue can significantly hinder meditation. Scripture acknowledges the body's influence on spiritual practice, as when Jesus found His disciples sleeping because "their eyes were heavy" (Matt. 26:43).

Physical discomfort, restlessness, or fatigue can significantly hinder meditation. Scripture acknowledges the body's influence on spiritual practice, as when Jesus found His disciples sleeping because "their eyes were heavy" (Matthew 26:43).

**Breath-Enhanced Response**: Use your breath to establish body-spirit integration when physical challenges arise. Conscious breathing naturally calms the nervous system and reduces physical tension. Rather than fighting against bodily sensations, breathe into them with acceptance and awareness. The divine breath that formed your physical body understands its limitations and needs. Each conscious breath honors the body as the temple of the Holy Spirit (1 Corinthians 6:19) while gently inviting it into alignment with spiritual practice. This breath-centered body awareness helps fulfill Paul's desire that "your whole spirit, soul and body be kept blameless" (1 Thessalonians 5:23).

## 4. Emotional Resistance

Emotional states—anxiety, boredom, frustration, apathy— often create resistance to meditation. Scripture acknowledges these emotional realities, as David asks himself, **"Why, my soul, are you downcast? Why so disturbed within me?" (Psalm 42:5).**

**Breath-Enhanced Response**: When emotional resistance arises, use your breath as a compassionate response rather than forcing yourself to "feel" differently. With each inhalation, acknowledge the emotion without judgment; with each exhalation, create space around it rather than being controlled by it.

The divine breath that animated your emotional capacity understands its complexities. Each conscious breath creates what early Christian writers called apatheia—not absence of emotion but freedom from being dominated by emotional states. This breath-centered emotional awareness fulfills Paul's instruction to "not be anxious about anything" (Philippians 4:6) by providing a pathway through anxiety rather than a denial of it.

## 5. Isolation

Attempting to maintain any spiritual discipline without community support increases vulnerability to discouragement and inconsistency. Scripture consistently emphasizes the communal context of spiritual formation: **"And let us consider how we may spur one another on toward love and good deeds, not giving up meeting together, as some are in the habit of doing, but encouraging one another." Hebrews 10:24-25 (NIV)**

**Breath-Enhanced Response**: When isolation threatens your practice, remember that the same divine breath dwells in all believers, creating spiritual connection even when physical gathering isn't possible. Your conscious breathing connects you to this shared reality—the communion of saints united by one spirit.

The divine breath (Pneuma) that formed the church at Pentecost continues to unite believers across time and space. Each conscious breath becomes an opportunity to inhale awareness of this spiritual community and exhale the illusion of isolated practice. This breath-centered communion fulfills Jesus's **prayer "that all of them may be one, Father, just as you are in me, and I am in you" (John 17:21).**

# 6. Spiritual Opposition

Scripture acknowledges spiritual practices face opposition from forces that resist transformation: "For our struggle is not against flesh and blood, but against... the spiritual forces of evil in the heavenly realms" (Ephesians 6:12). This opposition often manifests as unusual obstacles, distractions, or discouragements when attempting to establish consistent meditation.

**Breath-Enhanced Response**: When spiritual opposition arises, your breath becomes a powerful reminder of the greater Spirit who dwells within you. As **1 John 4:4 affirms, "the one who is in you is greater than the one who is in the world."** Each conscious breath connects you to this indwelling power that overcomes all opposition.

The divine breath that empowered Jesus to overcome temptation in the wilderness now empowers you through every spiritual challenge. Each breath becomes an opportunity to inhale God's authority and exhale fear of opposition. This breath-centered spiritual authority fulfills

Jesus's promise: **"I have given you authority… to overcome all the power of the enemy" (Luke 10:19).**

Recognizing these challenges doesn't mean surrendering to them, but developing specific strategies to address them. Despite these obstacles, this chapter offers practical approaches to establishing a sustainable meditation practice.

# Creating Your Personal Meditation Plan

A sustainable meditation practice begins with a personalized plan that aligns with your unique circumstances, personality, and spiritual journey. This isn't about imposing rigid formulas, but developing a thoughtful structure that facilitates consistency.

## Assessing Your Current Reality

Begin by honestly assessing your present situation:

### 1. Time Inventory

Conduct a realistic inventory of your current time allocation: - Track how you spend time for several typical days - Identify patterns, including both fixed commitments and flexible time - Notice periods that might accommodate meditation practice - Recognize seasons or cycles in your schedule (e.g., academic terms, business quarters)

This inventory provides accurate data for planning rather than relying on assumptions about your schedule. As Jesus advised, **"Suppose one of you wants to build a tower.**

**Won't you first sit down and estimate the cost? Luke 14:28 (NIV)**

**Breath-Enhanced Application**: Conducting this inventory, use breath awareness to maintain honest self-perception. With each inhalation, invite clarity about how you spend time; with each exhalation, release idealized or distorted perceptions. This breath-centered honesty creates a foundation for realistic planning.

## 2. Energy Mapping

Beyond time availability, consider your energy patterns: - When are you naturally most alert and focused? - When do you typically experience energy dips? - How do these patterns align with potential meditation times? - What factors affect your energy levels (e.g., sleep, nutrition, stress)?

This mapping helps schedule meditation when you're most capable of focused attention, rather than when you're likely to struggle with fatigue or distraction.

**Breath-Enhanced Application**: Your breath provides valuable feedback about energy levels. Throughout the day, pause for three conscious breaths at different times, noticing the quality of your breathing—is it deep and easy or shallow and strained? This breath awareness reveals your natural energy rhythms for optimal meditation scheduling.

## 3. Personality Assessment

Consider how your personality affects your approach to spiritual practices: - Are you naturally drawn to structure or spontaneity? - Do you prefer intellectual, emotional, or physical engagement? - Are you energized or drained by social interaction? - How do you typically respond to expectations (meeting, resisting, or exceeding them)?

This assessment helps customize your meditation plan to work with rather than against your natural tendencies, increasing sustainability.

**Breath-Enhanced Application**: Your breathing patterns often reflect personality tendencies. Do you naturally breathe in a structured, rhythmic pattern or more variable, spontaneous way? This breath awareness provides clues about designing a meditation approach that honors your God-given personality while gently stretching you toward growth.

## 4. Spiritual Season Discernment

Reflect on your current spiritual season: - Are you in a period of growth, testing, transition, or consolidation? - What specific aspects of meditation seem most relevant to this season? - What spiritual hunger or need feels most pressing right now? - How might God invite you to adjust spiritual practices for this season?

This discernment aligns your meditation practice with God's current work rather than imposing practices that might be more appropriate for different seasons.

**Breath-Enhanced Application**: Your breath often reveals your spiritual season. Is your breathing anxious and shallow (perhaps showing a testing season), deep and peaceful (consolidation), or somewhere between? Use this breath awareness to discern your spiritual climate and design meditation practices accordingly.

[254]

# Designing Your Customized Plan

Based on this assessment, design a meditation plan with these components:

## 1. Frequency and Duration

Determine realistic frequency and duration for your practice: - Start with what's sustainable rather than what's impressive - Consider beginning with brief daily sessions (5-10 minutes) rather than longer weekly ones - Plan gradual increases as the practice becomes established - Include both regular brief sessions and occasional extended ones.

Remember Jesus's teaching about faithfulness in small things: **"Whoever can be trusted with very little can also be trusted with much" (Luke 16:10)**. Starting with manageable commitments builds confidence and momentum for growth.

**Breath-Enhanced Application**: Use your breath as a natural timer for meditation duration. Rather than watching a clock, which can create anxiety, consider measuring sessions by breath cycles—perhaps starting with 20-30 conscious breaths. This breath-based timing honors your body's natural rhythm while maintaining consistent practice.

## 2. Timing and Location

Identify specific times and places for meditation: - Select times that align with your energy patterns and schedule realities - Choose locations that minimize distractions and support focus - Consider creating environmental cues that signal meditation time (e.g., a specific chair, candle, or background music) - Plan alternative times and places for days when primary options aren't available.

This specificity increases follow-through by removing decision fatigue and creating environmental support. As Jesus showed by regularly withdrawing to "solitary places" (Luke 5:16), physical location significantly affects spiritual practice.

**Breath-Enhanced Application**: Different environments affect your breathing patterns. Notice how your breath feels in various potential meditation locations—where does it naturally deepen and slow? These locations likely provide optimal conditions for meditation. Similarly, notice times of day when your breathing is naturally calmer and more regular—these often show ideal meditation times.

## 3. Content and Focus

Determine what specific meditation practices you'll engage: - Select practices aligned with your current spiritual needs and season - Consider rotating through different meditations rather than using only one approach - Identify specific Scriptures or themes for initial focus - Plan how to track insights or questions that arise during meditation.

This content planning prevents the paralysis of meditating without clear direction. As Proverbs teaches, **"The plans of the diligent lead to profit" (Proverbs 21:5).**

**Breath-Enhanced Application**: Different meditation content affects your breathing in unique ways. Scripture meditation might produce steady, rhythmic breathing; contemplative prayer might lead to deeper, slower breathing, while intercessory prayer might create more variable patterns. Notice these connections and use them to select practices that best serve your current spiritual needs.

## 4. Accountability and Support

Establish structures for accountability and support: - Identify at least one person who will regularly ask about your practice - Consider joining or forming a meditation group that meets periodically - Determine how you'll track your consistency (journal, app, calendar) - Plan how you'll respond to inevitable inconsistency (grace-filled restart rather than abandonment).

This relational component acknowledges sustainable spiritual practices rarely develop in isolation. As Ecclesiastes observes, "Two are better than one... If either of them falls, one can help the other up" (Ecclesiastes 4:9-10).

**Breath-Enhanced Application**: Shared breathing creates a powerful connection in a spiritual community. Meeting with accountability partners or meditation groups involves several minutes of conscious breathing together. This shared breath awareness acknowledges that the same divine breath (Pneuma) dwells in each believer, creating unity that strengthens individual practice.

# Integrating Meditation into Daily Life

Beyond formal meditation sessions, sustainability develops through integration with daily life. Jesus modeled this integration, maintaining communion with the Father amid active ministry rather than compartmentalizing spiritual practice.

[257]

## Breath-Centered Micro-Practices

Develop brief practices that can be integrated throughout your day:

## 1. Transition Moments

Use transitions between activities as opportunities for brief meditation: - Before starting your car, take three conscious breaths while inviting God's presence into your journey - When moving between meetings or tasks, pause for a breath-centered moment of recollection - Upon arriving home, breathe deeply for 30 seconds to transition from work to family presence - Before checking email or social media, take several breaths to establish centered intention.

These transition practices fulfill Paul's instruction to "pray continually" (1 Thessalonians 5:17) by integrating spiritual awareness throughout daily activities.

**Breath-Enhanced Application**: Transitions naturally affect breathing patterns, often creating shallow, rapid breathing as you rush from one activity to another. By consciously deepening and slowing your breath during transitions, you interrupt autopilot functioning and make space for God's presence in ordinary moments.

## 2. Waiting Opportunities

Transform waiting times into meditation opportunities: - While waiting in line, practice breath awareness instead of checking your phone - During hold times on phone calls, use breath to center in God's presence - While waiting for appointments, engage in brief Scripture meditation - When

[258]

stuck in traffic, practice gratitude with each breath rather than impatience.

These waiting practices fulfill Isaiah's promise that **"those who wait on the LORD shall renew their strength" (Isaiah 40:31),** transforming potential frustration into spiritual renewal.

**Breath-Enhanced Application**: Waiting situations typically trigger either shallow, anxious breathing (impatience) or sighing (resignation). By consciously engaging your breath during these times, you transform physiological stress responses into opportunities for spiritual connection. Each conscious breath while waiting becomes a mini meditation that accumulates throughout your day.

## 3. Task-Integrated Awareness

Infuse routine tasks with meditative awareness: - While washing dishes, synchronize your breathing with the washing motion, recognizing God's cleansing presence - During exercise, coordinate breath with movement as a form of embodied prayer - While walking between locations, match your breathing to your steps as walking meditation - During repetitive tasks, use breath to maintain God-awareness rather than mental wandering.

These integrated practices fulfill the monastic principle of finding God in ordinary work, as expressed in the Benedictine motto "Ora et Labora" (Prayer and Work).

**Breath-Enhanced Application**: Different tasks create different breathing patterns—some constrict breathing while others naturally deepen it. By bringing conscious awareness to your breath during routine activities, you transform physiological patterns that often reinforce stress or disconnection. Each breath-conscious task becomes an opportunity for practicing presence rather than mindless automation.

## Environmental Reminders

Create environmental cues that prompt meditation integration:

## 1. Visual Triggers

Place visual reminders in your regular environment: - Post small Scripture cards in frequently viewed locations (bathroom mirror, computer monitor, car dashboard) - Set phone lock screen or desktop wallpaper with meditation prompts - Wear or carry a small item (bracelet, pocket stone) that reminds you to breathe consciously - Position symbolic objects in your workspace that prompt spiritual recollection.

These visual triggers fulfill God's principle in Deuteronomy 6:8-9, where physical reminders (phylacteries, doorposts) prompted spiritual awareness.

**Breath-Enhanced Application**: When encountering these visual triggers, pause for three conscious breaths before continuing your activity. This brief breath awareness interrupts unconscious patterns and reestablishes connection with the divine breath. Over time, even glimpsing these reminders begins to deepen your breathing automatically.

## 2. Digital Notifications

Use technology as a meditation support rather than a distraction: Set recurring calendar reminders for brief meditation pauses, use meditation apps with scheduled reminders throughout the day, create custom alerts with meditation prompts or Scripture verses, and establish technology boundaries that protect meditation times.

These digital tools transform potential distractions into spiritual supports, fulfilling Paul's principle of bringing everything "into captivity to the obedience of Christ" (2 Corinthians 10:5)—even modern technology.

**Breath-Enhanced Application**: When digital notifications interrupt your activity, use them as opportunities for breath awareness rather than immediate task-switching. Three conscious breaths before responding to notifications creates space for discernment and presence rather than reactivity. This breath-centered pause gradually transforms your relationship with technology.

## 3. Relational Agreements

Establish agreements with close relationships that support meditation integration: - Create family rituals that include brief meditation elements (mealtime prayers, bedtime reflection) - Develop shared language about respecting meditation times - Establish communication norms that include pauses for presence - Invite appropriate others to participate in occasional meditation practices.

These relational agreements acknowledge that sustainable spiritual practices require support from close relationships rather than being isolated from them.

**Breath-Enhanced Application**: Shared breathing creates powerful connections in relationships. Before difficult conversations, suggest taking three breaths together. Before family meals, establish a brief shared breathing practice. These breath-centered moments create unity while reinforcing individual meditation practice, fulfilling Peter's instruction to "live in harmony with one another" (1 Peter 3:8).

# Overcoming Common Obstacles

Even with careful planning and integration strategies, obstacles to sustainable practice inevitably arise. Scripture acknowledges this reality while providing wisdom for overcoming challenges.

## Addressing Inconsistency

Perhaps the most common obstacle is inconsistency, beginning with enthusiasm but gradually tapering off in practice. Scripture acknowledges this tendency while encouraging perseverance: **"Let us not become weary in doing good, for at the proper time we will reap a harvest if we do not give up" (Galatians 6:9)**.

## 1. Grace-Based Restart

When inconsistency occurs (not if but when), practice grace-based restart: - Acknowledge the lapse without harsh self-judgment or shame - Identify factors that contributed to inconsistency without making excuses - Adjust your plan based on these insights rather than simply trying harder - Begin again with realistic expectations and self-compassion.

This approach embodies the gospel principle that growth occurs through grace rather than condemnation. As Paul writes, **"There is now no condemnation for those who are in Christ Jesus" (Romans 8:1).**

**Breath-Enhanced Application**: When you notice an inconsistency in your practice, use your breath to process this reality without shame. Inhale God's unconditional acceptance; exhale self-condemnation. Inhale fresh commitment; exhale discouragement about past lapses. This breath-centered processing creates emotional conditions for a sustainable restart rather than abandonment.

## 2. Minimum Viable Practice

Establish a "minimum viable practice" for challenging periods: - Determine the absolute minimum meditation commitment you'll maintain even in busiest times - Make this minimum so achievable that it eliminates excuses (e.g., three conscious breaths morning and evening) - Commit to this minimum regardless of circumstances, while doing more when possible - Recognize that maintained connection through minimal practice during difficult seasons is success, not failure.

This approach acknowledges human limitations while maintaining continuous practice. As Jesus taught, faithfulness in "very little" matters more than sporadic grand gestures (Luke 16:10).

**Breath-Enhanced Application**: Your breath is always available, making it the perfect foundation for minimum viable practice. You can take three fully conscious breaths even in the busiest or most challenging circumstances. This breath awareness, though brief, maintains your connection to the divine breath and preserves the habit of meditation even when extended practice isn't possible.

## 3. Progress Tracking

Implement simple systems for tracking meditation consistency: - Use a method that provides visual feedback on your practice pattern - Consider apps designed for habit tracking, a simple calendar, or journal - Record not only consistency but also insights, challenges, and adjustments - Review your tracking periodically to identify patterns and progress.

This tracking creates accountability and motivation while providing data for refinement. As Proverbs advises, "Know well the condition of your flocks" (Proverbs 27:23, ESV)—including your spiritual practices. Breath-Enhanced Application: When reviewing your tracking records, use breath awareness to process your observations without judgment. Inhale objective awareness; exhale both pride and shame. This breath-centered review creates conditions for honest assessment and appropriate adjustments rather than discouragement or complacency.

## Managing Expectations

Unrealistic expectations frequently undermine sustainable practice. Scripture acknowledges the importance of proper expectations, as when Jesus taught His disciples to anticipate both difficulty and fruit in the spiritual journey (John 16:33; John 15:5).

## 1. Recognizing Common Misconceptions

Identify and address common meditation misconceptions: - Meditation always produces immediate peace or insight (in reality, experiences vary widely) - Consistent meditators never experience wandering thoughts (in fact, this is universal) - Spiritual growth through meditation follows a steady, linear progression (in fact, growth includes plateaus and even apparent regression) - "Successful" meditation means achieving certain mental or emotional states (in reality, success is showing up consistently regardless of experiences)

Addressing these misconceptions prevents discouragement when reality doesn't match idealized expectations.

**Breath-Enhanced Application:** When you notice expectation-reality gaps in your meditation experience, use your breath to create space for acceptance. Inhale what is happening; exhale what you think should be happening. This breath-centered acceptance aligns you with reality rather than ideals, creating conditions for authentic practice rather than performance-based spirituality.

## 2. Embracing the Desert

Prepare for spiritual dryness as usual rather than exceptional: - Study Scripture's desert experiences (Jesus, Elijah, John the Baptist, Israel) as essential rather than optional - Recognize that feelings of God's absence often accompany spiritual growth rather than indicating failure - Develop specific strategies for maintaining practice during perceived spiritual dryness - View these seasons as opportunities for purifying motivation and deepening faith.

This preparation fulfills Jesus's teaching to "build your house on the rock" (Matthew 7:24) so that it withstands inevitable storms rather than collapsing when challenges arise.

**Breath-Enhanced Application**: During spiritual dryness, your breath becomes an important anchor. When feelings and experiences seem absent, the rhythm of your breathing provides a tangible connection to the divine breath that remains present regardless of perceptions. Each conscious breath during desert seasons becomes an act of faith, trusting God's presence even when not emotionally experienced.

## 3. Celebrating Small Victories

Develop practices for noticing and celebrating incremental progress: - Identify specific markers of growth beyond feelings (increased Scripture knowledge, behavioral changes, perspective shifts) - Regularly acknowledge these small victories through gratitude practices - Share progress with trusted companions who can affirm growth you might miss - Record evidence of transformation to review during discouraging periods.

This celebration fulfills Paul's instruction to "rejoice in the Lord always" (Philippians 4:4) by cultivating attention to God's ongoing work rather than focusing exclusively on shortcomings or goals not yet reached.

**Breath-Enhanced Application**: Use your breath as a vehicle for celebration and gratitude. When noticing even small growth, inhale awareness of God's faithfulness; exhale praise and thanksgiving. This breath-centered celebration reinforces continued practice while fulfilling the biblical pattern of acknowledging God's work: "Praise the LORD, my soul, and forget not all his benefits" (Psalm 103:2).

## Adapting Through Different Seasons.

Life circumstances inevitably change, requiring adaptation of spiritual practices. Scripture acknowledges these changing seasons: "There is a time for everything, and a season for every activity under the heavens" (Ecclesiastes 3:1).

# 1. Life Transitions

Develop strategies for maintaining practice through significant life transitions: - Anticipate how transitions (job changes, moves, relationship shifts, health changes) will affect your meditation routine - Proactively adjust your plan before transitions rather than waiting until patterns are broken - Temporarily simplify practice during major transitions rather than abandoning it - Establish new patterns as quickly as possible once circumstances stabilize.

This proactive adaptation prevents the typical pattern of practice cessation during transitions. As Proverbs advises, "The prudent see danger and take refuge" (Proverbs 22:3) rather than being caught unprepared.

**Breath-Enhanced Application**: During transitions, your breath provides continuity amid change. When everything else is in flux, your breathing is constantly connected to God's presence. By maintaining breath awareness during transitions, you preserve the essence of meditation practice even when specific forms must change. Each conscious breath becomes a portable sanctuary in changing circumstances.

# 2. Spiritual Seasons

Recognize and adapt to different spiritual seasons: - Identify your current spiritual season (consolation, desolation, purgation, illumination) through reflection and spiritual direction - Adjust meditation content and approach to align with this season's needs - Recognize that different seasons require different metrics for "success" - Trust God's wisdom in guiding you through various seasons rather than attempting to control the process This seasonal awareness fulfills the biblical pattern of discerning God's timing, as exemplified by the sons of Issachar, **"who understood the times and knew what Israel should do" (1 Chronicles 12:32).**

**Breath-Enhanced Application**: Different spiritual seasons create different breathing patterns—consolation often produces deep, peaceful breathing; desolation may create constricted breathing; purgation might involve sighing; illumination could generate breathless awe. By noticing these breath patterns without judgment, you gain valuable information about your spiritual season and can adapt your practice accordingly.

## 3. Physical Limitations

Develop adaptations for physical circumstances that affect meditation: - Create modified practices for illness, injury, or chronic conditions - Adjust expectations and methods during high fatigue or stress periods - Explore how physical limitations might actually deepen rather than hinder practice - View the body as a partner rather than an obstacle in spiritual formation.

This adaptation acknowledges Paul's experience of finding God's strength perfected in weakness (2 Corinthians 12:9) rather than requiring perfect physical conditions for spiritual practice.

**Breath-Enhanced Application**: Physical limitations often affect breathing patterns, which can enhance meditation when approached mindfully. Illness that slows breathing, pain that makes breathing conscious, or limitations that require breath management create heightened breath awareness that can deepen spiritual connection. Each breath amid physical limitation becomes an opportunity to experience God's presence in weakness rather than only in strength.

# The Role of Community in Sustainable Practice

While meditation involves personal discipline, Scripture consistently emphasizes the communal context of spiritual formation. Proverbs observes, **"As iron sharpens iron, so one person sharpens another" (Proverbs 27:17).**

## Finding or Creating a Meditation Community

Identify or develop community support for your practice:

### 1. Existing Communities

Explore potential communities that might support meditation practice: Church small groups or Sunday school classes interested in contemplative practices, retreat centers or spiritual formation organizations in your area, online communities focused on Christian meditation, and friends or family members with similar spiritual interests.

This exploration acknowledges that God often provides resources we overlook. As Genesis records, "Surely the LORD is in this place, and I was not aware of it" (Genesis 28:16).

**Breath-Enhanced Application**: When exploring potential communities, use your breath as a discernment tool. Notice how your breathing responds in different groups—does it naturally deepen and slow, showing resonance, or become shallow and tense, suggesting caution? This breath awareness provides valuable intuitive information about community fit beyond intellectual assessment.

## 2. Creating Simple Structures

If existing communities aren't available, create simple structures: - Invite one or two friends to meet monthly for shared meditation and discussion - Establish a regular video call with geographically distant meditation partners - Propose a meditation component within existing church groups - Create an email or text group for sharing meditation insights and encouragement.

This creation fulfills Jesus's promise that **"where two or three gather in my name, there am I with them" (Matthew 18:20)**—even in the simplest community structures.

**Breath-Enhanced Application**: When gathering with others for meditation, begin with several minutes of conscious breathing together before speaking. This shared breath awareness acknowledges that the same divine breath (Pneuma) dwells in each person, creating a unity that transcends differences. Each shared breath becomes a wordless communion that strengthens individual practice and community bonds.

## 3. Spiritual Direction

Consider working with a spiritual director: - Research spiritual directors in your area or available for remote sessions - Interview potential directors to assess compatibility with your tradition and needs - Establish regular meetings (typically monthly) for reflection on your meditation journey - Use these conversations for accountability, discernment, and adjustment of practices.

This relationship provides personalized guidance from someone experienced in spiritual formation. As Proverbs advises, **"The way of fools seems right to them, but the wise listen to advice" (Proverbs 12:15).**

**Breath-Enhanced Application**: During spiritual direction sessions, notice your breathing patterns when discussing different aspects of your practice. Constricted breathing often indicates areas needing attention, while easy, deep breathing may reveal authentic growth. This breath awareness provides valuable information for both you and your director about your spiritual journey beyond what words alone convey.

## Communal Practices

Develop specific practices that combine personal meditation with community support:

## 1. Group Meditation

Establish regular group meditation gatherings: - Begin with simple formats—shared silence, lectio divina, or guided meditation - Include brief sharing of experiences and insights after meditation periods - Rotate leadership responsibilities to develop multiple facilitators - Maintain focus on practice rather than merely discussing meditation.

These gatherings fulfill the early church pattern of meeting together for prayer (Acts 1:14; 2:42) while providing mutual encouragement in spiritual disciplines.

**Breath-Enhanced Application**: In group meditation, the sound of others breathing creates a powerful reminder of the shared spiritual journey. Rather than finding this distracting, use awareness of others' breathing to deepen your practice—each breath you hear becomes a reminder of the divine breath animating all believers. This breath-centered community awareness fulfills Paul's image of the church as one body with many parts (1 Corinthians 12:12-27).

## 2. Accountability Partnerships

Establish specific accountability relationships: - Identify one or two people who will regularly ask about your meditation practice - Determine specific questions they'll ask and how you'll respond - Schedule regular check-ins (in person, phone, or text) at agreed intervals - Balance accountability with grace to avoid legalism or shame.

These partnerships fulfill James's instruction to **"confess your sins to each other and pray for each other so that you may be healed" (James 5:16)** by creating specific structures for mutual support.

**Breath-Enhanced Application:** When discussing your practice with accountability partners, use breath awareness to maintain honesty and vulnerability. Before responding to questions, take three conscious breaths to move beyond surface answers or defensiveness. This breath-centered communication creates conditions for authentic sharing rather than performance-based reporting.

## 3. Retreats and Intensives

Participate in periodic retreats or intensive experiences: If possible, Schedule at least one meditation-focused retreat annually. Consider both guided group retreats and personal silent retreats. Use these experiences to deepen practice, receive teaching, and reset habits. Develop specific strategies for integrating retreat insights into daily life. Check out Christian Meditation Academy's website for the latest workshops and retreats.

These concentrated experiences fulfill Jesus's pattern of periodically withdrawing from activity for extended communion with the Father (Luke 6:12; Mark 1:35).

**Breath-Enhanced Application**: Retreats provide unique opportunities for extended breath awareness beyond what daily life typically allows. Use this expanded time to explore different breathing patterns and their effects on your meditation experience. Notice how several days of conscious breathing gradually shift your awareness and presence. These insights can then inform your ongoing practice after returning to regular routines.

# Conclusion: The Lifelong Breath of Meditation

As we conclude our exploration of establishing a sustainable meditation practice, remember that the breath of life flowing through you right now is not merely biological respiration,

# CHAPTER FOURTEEN:
## Establishing A Sustainable
## Meditation Practice

but a continuous invitation to communion with God. Each breath you take carries the potential for renewed commitment to the meditation journey—whether in dedicated sessions, brief daily moments, or communal gatherings.

The Hebrew understanding of Neshama and the Greek concept of Pneuma reveal that God has designed your breathing to be a sustainable connection to His presence. This isn't mystical imagination but biblical reality—the same divine breath that first animated humanity continues to sustain spiritual practice in those who respond to its gentle rhythm.

As you develop your meditation practice, let each conscious breath remind you of Jesus's promise: **"I am with you always, to the very end of the age" (Matthew 28:20**). The divine breath within you is not temporary but eternal, not fragile but resilient, not limited but continuously available to sustain your spiritual journey through every season and circumstance.

In the final chapter, we'll explore how to share the gift of Christian meditation with others, extending the benefits you've experienced to family, friends, church communities, and beyond. This sharing dimension completes the cycle of receiving and giving that characterizes authentic spiritual formation in the way of Christ.

## CHAPTER FIFTEEN:
# Sharing the Gift Of Christian Meditation

Don't keep the transformative power of Christian meditation to yourself. As you've experienced the profound benefits of connecting with God through meditation, you're now positioned to share this gift with others. Jesus commissioned His followers to practice His teachings and "teach all nations" (Matt. 28:19-20). This chapter explores how to effectively share Christian meditation with individuals and groups in ways that honor both the practice and the people you're teaching.

At the heart of sharing Christian meditation is the divine breath of life—the same *ruach, neshama, and pneuma* woven throughout this book. This divine breath is the perfect entry point for introducing others to meditation, providing a universal, accessible foundation that transcends backgrounds and experience levels. Just as God breathed life into humanity at creation, this same breath becomes the bridge through which others can experience the living presence of God in meditation.

# Understanding Different Starting Points

People approach Christian meditation from diverse backgrounds, each with unique needs, concerns, and expectations. Recognizing these different starting points helps you tailor your approach effectively.

## The Divine Breath as Universal Connection Point

Before exploring specific audience types, it's essential to recognize how the breath of life is a universal connection point for everyone, regardless of background. Every person breathes approximately 20,000 times daily—a continuous reminder of our dependence on God and connection to divine life. This universal experience provides the perfect foundation for introducing Christian meditation.

The breath serves as:

- **Common Human Experience**: Everyone breathes, making breath awareness an accessible starting point regardless of religious background or meditation experience.

- **Biblical Connection**: The breath directly connects to Scripture's teaching about God's life-giving spirit (Gen. 2:7, Job 33:4, Ezek. 37:5).

- **Physical-Spiritual Bridge**: Breath awareness naturally bridges physical relaxation benefits with deeper spiritual dimensions.

[276]

- **Non-Threatening Entry Point**: Beginning with breath observation feels safe and accessible even to those skeptical of religious practices.

With this universal foundation in mind, let's explore how to adapt your approach to different audiences while keeping the divine breath central to your teaching.

## 1.   The Spiritually Curious

Some people approach meditation primarily for its practical benefits.

They may:

- Seek stress reduction or personal growth.

- Have exposure to secular or Eastern meditation approaches.

- Lack of familiarity with Christian terminology and concepts.

- Be open to spiritual experience but wary of religious institutions.

For these individuals, Christian meditation offers an accessible entry point to authentic spirituality that can eventually lead to broader Christian faith. Jesus often began with people's felt needs before addressing deeper spiritual realities, as with the woman at the well (John 4:1-26).

**Breath-Enhanced Approach**: With the spiritually curious, begin by introducing breath awareness as a scientifically validated practice for stress reduction and mental clarity. As they grow comfortable with this foundation, gradually introduce the concept of breath as a divine gift—the neshama that connects us to our Creator. Share how conscious breathing creates space for experiencing God's presence without requiring complex theological frameworks. This breath-centered approach creates a natural bridge between physical benefits and spiritual depth.

## 2.  The Traditionally Religious

Others come from traditional Christian backgrounds, but have never explored contemplative practices. They may:

- Have strong doctrinal foundations but limited experiential dimensions.

- Feel skeptical about meditation because of associations with other religions.

- Value Scripture but approach it primarily intellectually rather than formally.

- Worry about whether meditation aligns with their denominational tradition.

For these individuals, Christian meditation offers a way to deepen their existing faith through experiential engagement while remaining rooted in biblical truth. Paul addressed this need for experiential knowledge when he prayed believers might **"know this love that surpasses knowledge" (Eph. 3:19).**

**Breath-Enhanced Approach:** With traditionally religious individuals, begin with the rich biblical theology of breath, showing how *ruach* appears nearly 400 times in Scripture and connects directly to God's Spirit. Help them see breath meditation as deeply biblical rather than foreign by exploring passages like Genesis 2:7, Ezekiel 37, and John 20:22, where God's breath brings life, renewal, and empowerment. Demonstrate how breath-centered prayer enhances rather than replaces traditional spiritual disciplines, deepening their connection to familiar practices like Bible study and worship.

### 3. The Spiritually Wounded

- Some approach meditation after experiencing hurt within religious contexts. They may:

- Carry wounds from legalistic or controlling religious environments

- Feel ambivalent about Christian terminology and institutions

- Desire authentic spirituality without manipulative elements

- Need healing before they can fully engage with the Christian community

For these individuals, Christian meditation offers a gentle path back to God that emphasizes direct relationship rather than institutional requirements. As Isaiah prophesied, Jesus showed special tenderness toward the wounded: **"A bruised reed he will not break, and a smoldering wick he will not snuff out" (Isa. 42:3).**

**Breath-Enhanced Approach**: With the spiritually wounded, the divine breath offers a gentle, non-threatening reintroduction to God's presence. Begin by emphasizing how breath meditation creates a safe space for healing, each breath becoming a reminder that God sustains them, regardless of past religious experiences. The rhythm of breathing in God's love and breathing out pain provides a tangible practice for processing spiritual wounds. Gradually, we will introduce the concept of pneuma as the comforting, healing presence of God that works through their breath, which is distinct from institutional religion.

### 4.   The Analytically Minded

Some approach meditation primarily with an intellectual interest. They may:

- Want to understand the historical and theological foundations before practicing.

- Question the scientific validity or measurable benefits.

- Need logical frameworks to organize their understanding.

- Process experiences through analytical rather than intuitive faculties.

For these individuals, Christian meditation offers both intellectual depth and experiential richness, satisfying both dimensions of engagement. Jesus honored this analytical approach when He invited Thomas to examine His wounds (John 20:27), meeting intellectual needs while inviting deeper faith.

**Breath-Enhanced Approach**: With analytical individuals, present the breath of life concept through both scientific and theological lenses. Share research on how breath awareness affects the nervous system and brain function, then connect these findings to the Hebrew and Greek understandings of breath in Scripture. Explore the linguistic connections between *ruach*, *neshama*, and *pneuma*, showing how these concepts developed throughout biblical history. This intellectual framework provides a solid foundation for their practice while honoring their need for comprehensive understanding.

## 5.  The Already Contemplative

Some already practice contemplative prayer or meditation within the Christian tradition. They may:

- Have experience with specific approaches like Lectio Divina or centering prayer.

- Seek to broaden their practice with additional methods.

- Desire a deeper understanding of biblical and theological foundations.

- Want to connect individual practice with community dimensions.

For these individuals, the practices in this book offer complementary approaches that enrich their contemplative life. Paul affirms this building upon existing foundations: **"I planted the seed, Apollos watered it, but God has been making it grow" (1 Cor. 3:6).**

**Breath-Enhanced Approach**: With experienced contemplatives, explore the nuanced dimensions of breath theology that might enhance their practice. Introduce the Hebrew letter study of *ruach* (רוּחַ) to reveal deeper spiritual meanings. Share how conscious breathing can be integrated with their familiar practices—adding breath awareness to Lectio Divina, using breath as an anchor in centering prayer, or synchronizing breath with prayer movements. This approach honors their experience while offering fresh dimensions through the divine breath perspective.

By discerning someone's starting point, you can tailor your introduction to Christian meditation to address their specific needs, concerns, and learning styles. This discernment follows Jesus's example of meeting each person in their unique circumstance while inviting them to greater spiritual depth.

# Introducing Meditation
# to Individuals

When sharing Christian meditation with individuals—whether family members, friends, colleagues, or others—several principles can guide a practical introduction:

### 1.  Begin with Your Personal Experience

Rather than presenting meditation as an abstract concept or technique, share how it has affected your own spiritual journey:

- Describe specific ways meditation has deepened your relationship with God.

- Share authentic stories of both breakthroughs and challenges in your practice.

- Explain how meditation has affected your daily life, relationships, and faith.

- Avoid exaggeration or promises of dramatic results.

Breath-Enhanced Application: Share a specific story about how breath awareness has transformed a moment of anxiety, distraction, or spiritual dryness. Describe how connecting with the divine breath helped you experience God's presence in that moment. Personal testimony about breath, as the spiritual connection, is often more interesting than theoretical explanations.

[283]

## 2.    Offer a Simple Experience

After sharing your experience, invite the person to a brief, accessible meditation experience:

- Keep the first experience short (3-5 minutes).

- Use simple, clear language without jargon.

- Provide enough guidance to make them comfortable.

- Include Scripture to ground the experience biblically.

**Breath-Enhanced Application**: Guide them through a simple breath awareness practice: "For the next few minutes, simply notice your breath—God's gift of life flowing in and out. As you breathe in, receive God's presence; as you breathe out, release any tension or distraction. Remember Jesus's words: **'Peace I leave with you; my peace I give you' (John 14:27).** This breath-centered introduction provides an immediate, tangible meditation experience without overwhelming them with technique.

## 3.    Address Questions and Concerns

After the experience, create sacred space for questions and concerns:

- Listen attentively without defensiveness.

- Acknowledge the validity of their questions.

- Provide biblical and historical context.

- Distinguish Christian meditation from other forms when necessary.

**Breath-Enhanced Application**: When addressing concerns about meditation's origins or spiritual safety, the breath of life provides a robust biblical foundation. Explain how breath awareness is Christian, rooted in Genesis, where God breathes life into humanity, continued in Ezekiel's vision of breath reviving dry bones, and fulfilled in John, where Jesus breathes the Holy Spirit on his disciples. This breath-centered explanation grounds meditation firmly in Christian tradition.

4. **Provide Next Steps**

- For those interested in exploring further, offer appropriate next steps:

- Suggest specific practices matched to their needs and interests

- Recommend accessible resources (books, apps, videos)

- Invite them to join you for regular practice if appropriate

- Offer to be available for questions or guidance

**Breath-Enhanced Application**: Create a simple take-home guide with three breath-centered practices they can try during the week: (1) Morning breath prayer—inhaling "Lord Jesus" and exhaling "be with me today"; (2) Midday breath pause—three conscious breaths while remembering God's presence; (3) Evening breath review—breathing deeply while reflecting on moments they sensed God's presence that day. This breath-focused approach provides practical, memorable ways to integrate meditation into daily life.

# Facilitating Group Meditation

Sharing meditation in group settings—whether small gatherings, church classes, or retreats—presents both opportunities and challenges. Here are principles for effective group facilitation:

### 1. Create a Welcoming Environment

The physical and emotional environment significantly affects the meditation experience:

- Arrange the space to minimize distractions and maximize comfort.

- Consider lighting, temperature, seating, and acoustics.

- Establish a tone of acceptance and non-judgment.

- Address potential concerns or questions before beginning.

**Breath-Enhanced Application**: Begin group sessions with a simple breath awareness exercise that helps participants transition from external busyness to internal awareness. Guide them to notice how the room breathes together—a physical reminder of our shared dependence on God's breath of life and our connection as one body in Christ. This breath-centered beginning creates both individual centering and group cohesion.

## 2. Provide Clear Guidance

Groups typically need more explicit guidance than individuals:

- Explain what will happen before it happens.

- Use a warm, measured tone when leading.

- Include periods of silence, but not so long as to create anxiety.

- Offer alternatives for those with different needs or abilities.

**Breath-Enhanced Application**: Frame your guidance around the breath as an anchor to which participants can always return when distracted or uncertain. For example: "Throughout our time together, your breath remains a constant true companion—God's gift flowing in and out. Whenever you feel lost or distracted, return your attention to this breath, knowing it connects you to God's presence." This breath-centered guidance provides security and orientation throughout the experience.

### 3. Balance Structure and Flexibility

Effective group facilitation requires both a clear structure and adaptability:

- Have a planned flow but be willing to adjust based on group needs.

- Balance teaching, practice, and discussion.

- Read the group's liveliness and adjust timing accordingly.

- Allow space for unexpected moments of insight or connection.

Breath-Enhanced Application: Use the natural rhythm of breathing as a model for group flow, alternating between periods of input (inhale) and reflection (exhale). For example, after teaching a concept, guide the group to take several conscious breaths to absorb and integrate the teaching before moving on. This breath-synchronized approach creates a natural pacing that honors both learning and integration.

### 4. Foster Community While Respecting Individual Experience

Group meditation balances communal and personal dimensions:

- Create opportunities for shared experience without forcing participation

[288]

- Invite but don't require sharing of personal insights

- Acknowledge the diversity of experiences within the group

- Connect individual practice to community formation

**Breath-Enhanced Application**: Incorporate a "breath communion" practice where participants consciously breathe together for several minutes, recognizing how we share the same air and divine breath that sustains all life. An invitation can follow this to share briefly how they experienced God's presence through this shared breath. This practice tangibly shows how the divine breath honors individual experience and creates community connection.

# Addressing Common Concerns

When sharing Christian meditation, you'll likely encounter questions and concerns. Here are constructive ways to address common issues:

## 1. "Is Meditation Biblical?"

Some may question whether meditation aligns with Scripture:

- Point to biblical examples of meditation (Josh. 1:8, Ps. 1:2, Ps. 119:15)

- Distinguish Christian meditation (filling with God's truth) from other forms

- Explain how meditation deepens rather than replaces Bible study

- Share how early Christians practiced contemplative prayer

**Breath-Enhanced Response**: Scripture connects breath and spiritual life throughout the Bible. In Genesis 2:7, God breathed life into humanity. In Ezekiel 37, God's breath revives dry bones. In John 20:22, Jesus breathed the Holy Spirit on his disciples. When we practice breath awareness in meditation, we connect with this biblical understanding of breath as the vehicle of God's life and presence. Far from being non-biblical, breath meditation helps us experience the very breath of God described throughout Scripture.

## 2. "Is This Just Eastern Meditation Repackaged?"

Some may worry about the origins or influences of meditation practices:

- Acknowledge that many traditions include a meditation

- Clarify the distinct Christ-centered focus of Christian meditation

- Explain that techniques (like breath awareness) are neutral tools

- Christian meditation is rich in biblical content

**Breath-Enhanced Response: "While many traditions recognize the value of breath awareness, Christian breath meditation uniquely centers on the biblical understanding of breath as God's life-giving spirit.** When we focus on our breath in Christian meditation, we're not emptying ourselves but realizing God's presence within us through His breath of life. The Hebrew concept of *ruach* and the Greek concept of *pneuma* reveal that God's Spirit works through our breath—a distinctly biblical understanding that transforms a physical technique into spiritual communion."

## 3. "Isn't Meditation Just Navel-Gazing?"

Some may see meditation as self-absorbed or escapist:

- Explain how meditation cultivates awareness of God, not just self

- Share how meditation should lead to more engaged, compassionate action

- Connect contemplation with Jesus's rhythm of solitude and service

- Provide examples of how meditation has inspired social engagement

**Breath-Enhanced Response**: "Far from being self-absorbed, breath meditation connects us more deeply with God and others. We recognize our dependence and connection to all creation when we realize our breath as God's gift. The same divine breath (*ruach*) that sustains us also fills everyone. This awareness naturally leads to greater compassion and service. Jesus withdrew for prayer and returned to serve others with renewed power. Similarly, breath meditation helps us receive God's life so we can share it with others—it's about breathing in God's presence so we can breathe out God's love to the world."

## 4. "I Can't Stop My Thoughts—What Am I Doing Wrong?"

Many beginners feel frustrated by mental activity during meditation:

Normalize the experience of mental chatter. Explain that the goal isn't to stop thoughts, but to change our relationship to them. Offer practical strategies for working with distractions.

Emphasize progress over perfection.

**Breath-Enhanced Response**: "Having thoughts during meditation is completely normal—it's what minds do! The key is using your breath as an anchor. When you notice your mind wandering, return your attention to your breath—God's gift flowing in and out. Each return is a moment of spiritual growth, not failure. Think of it like spiritual weightlifting: each time you notice a distraction and return to your breath, you strengthen your spiritual attention muscle. The divine breath (*neshama*) remains constant even when our thoughts fluctuate, providing a stable connection to God's presence regardless of mental activity."

# Developing as a Meditation Guide

If you feel called to share meditation more extensively, consider these principles for growth as a guide:

## 1.  Deepen Your Practice

The most effective teaching flows from authentic experience:

- Maintain a consistent personal meditation practice

- Seek guidance from experienced mentors or spiritual directors

- Attend retreats or workshops to expand your understanding

- Notice how your teaching reflects your practice

**Breath-Enhanced Application**: Develop a daily practice specifically focused on experiencing the divine breath in different contexts—morning quiet time, midday pause, evening reflection, and even during activities. Keep a journal of your breath-centered insights and experiences, noting how God's presence manifests through conscious breathing in various circumstances. This dedicated practice will enrich your ability to guide others authentically.

## 2.  Continue Learning

Practical guides remain lifelong students:

- Study both ancient and contemporary writings on Christian contemplation.

- Learn from diverse Christian traditions (Orthodox, Catholic, Protestant).

- Understand the scientific research on meditation's effects.

- Develop familiarity with various approaches and their applications.

**Breath-Enhanced Application**: Create a focused study plan exploring breath theology across Christian traditions—from the Desert Fathers and Mothers who practiced breath prayer to the Hesychast tradition in Orthodox Christianity to contemporary breath-centered practices. Compare how different traditions understand the connection between breath and spirit and integrate these insights into your teaching. This breath-specific knowledge will add depth and richness to your guidance.

## 3. Develop Teaching Skills

Effective meditation guidance requires specific communication abilities:

- Practice speaking in a clear, calming voice

- Learn to pace instructions and allow silence

- Develop language that is inclusive and accessible

- Receive feedback and adjust your approach accordingly

**Breath-Enhanced Application**: Record yourself guiding a breath meditation and listen critically to your pacing, tone, and clarity. Practice synchronizing your guidance with natural breathing rhythms, allowing participants time to inhale and exhale fully between instructions. Develop a repertoire of breath-centered language that connects physical experience with spiritual reality in accessible ways. This breath-synchronized communication creates a seamless experience for participants.

## 4. Honor the Sacred Trust

Guiding others in meditation is a position of spiritual responsibility:

- Maintain boundaries and ethical standards

- Respect the diversity of spiritual journeys

- Avoid manipulation or pressure tactics

- Recognize when someone needs additional support beyond meditation

**Breath-Enhanced Application**: Remember that in guiding breath meditation, you invite people into awareness of God's most intimate gift—the breath of life that sustains their existence. Honor this sacred dimension by creating safe, respectful environments where people can uniquely encounter God's presence through their breath. Avoid using breath practices manipulatively or claiming authority over another's spiritual experience. This reverent approach honors both the divine breath and the sacred dignity of each person.

# Conclusion: The Ripple Effect

You share Christian meditation with others and take part in a sacred ripple effect. Each person who discovers this practice becomes a channel through which others encounter God's transforming presence. Jesus compared the kingdom of God to a mustard seed that grows into a tree where birds can nest. (Matt. 13:31-32)—a small beginning with far-reaching impact.

The divine breath that first animated humanity continues to flow through each generation of believers, bringing life, healing, and transformation. By sharing breath-centered Christian meditation, you participate in this ongoing flow of God's life-giving Spirit. Each person who learns to connect with God through their breath becomes another channel through which the divine breath flows into a world gasping for spiritual oxygen.

As you faithfully share this gift, trust that the same breath that empowered creation, resurrection, and Pentecost continues its life-giving work—one breath, one person, one community at a time.

# SCHOLARLY AND LITERARY REFERENCES

## Science of Meditation

Newberg, A. (2018). *Neurotheology: How Science Can Enlighten Us About Spirituality*.
Columbia University Press.
Leaf, C. (2013). *Switch On Your Brain: The Key to Peak Happiness, Thinking, and Health*.
Baker Books.
HeartMath Institute. (2015). *Science of the Heart: Exploring the Role of the Heart in*
*Human Performance*. HeartMath Institute.
Benson, H. (1975). *The Relaxation Response*. William Morrow and Company.
Kabat-Zinn, J. (1990). *Full Catastrophe Living: Using the Wisdom of Your Body and Mind*
*to Face Stress, Pain, and Illness*. Delacorte Press.

## Christian Meditation and Spirituality
Winston, B. (2012). *The Missing Link of Meditation*. Bill Winston Ministries.
Stanley, C. (2017). *Finding Peace: God's Promise of a Life Free from Regret, Anxiety, and*
*Fear*. Thomas Nelson.
Nee, W. (1968). *The Spiritual Man*. Christian Fellowship Publishers.
Warren, R. (2002). *The Purpose Driven Life: What on Earth Am I Here For?* Zondervan.
Keller, T. (2016). *Prayer: Experiencing Awe and Intimacy with God*. Penguin Books.
à Kempis, T. (c. 1418-1427). *The Imitation of Christ*. Various publishers.

## Reference Works

Merriam-Webster. (2023). "Meditation." In *Merriam-Webster's Dictionary*. Retrieved from: https://www.merriam-webster.com/dictionary/meditation

American Psychological Association. (2023). "Meditation." In the *APA Dictionary of Psychology*. Retrieved from https://dictionary.apa.org/meditation

Oxford University Press. (2023). "Meditation." In the *Oxford English Dictionary*. Retrieved from https://www.oed.com/

Webster, N. (1828). "Meditation." In the *American Dictionary of the English Language*.

Retrieved from

http://webstersdictionary1828.com/Dictionary/meditation

# Christian Meditation Community

While individual practice forms the foundation of our spiritual discipline, the community powerfully sustains and deepens our meditation journey. Therefore, I've created the Christian Meditation Academy—not just a community, but the premier training ground for those seeking to master Christian meditation and potentially guide others on this transformative path.

As a member, you'll deepen your connection with the Holy Spirit through our comprehensive video courses on silent prayer and contemplative practice. Our meditative Bible study sessions offer a unique approach to Scripture, allowing you to engage with God's Word more profoundly and personally.

The Academy combines biblical principles with scientifically proven meditation techniques, ensuring a practical and authentically Christian experience centered entirely on the Holy Spirit. For those feeling called to share this gift with

[299]

others, we're excited to announce our upcoming Christian Meditation Instructor Certification program—a sacred opportunity to join the lineage of spiritual guides who have shared breath-centered practices throughout Christian history.

You'll learn to develop your teaching voice, master guiding others with appropriate pacing and silence, and honor the sacred trust of inviting others into awareness of God's most intimate gift—the breath of life. Through our community, you'll participate in the holy ripple effect Jesus described when comparing the kingdom to a mustard seed, as each person you guide potentially becomes another channel through which the divine breath flows into a world gasping for spiritual oxygen.

If you're seeking to transform your spiritual life, deepen your practice, or prepare to guide others, I invite you to visit **www.christianmeditationacademy.com** and **click** on the **Membership tab**. Together, we can launch our spiritual lives into the heavens and extend this life-giving practice to others—one breath, one person, one community at a time.

www.ingramcontent.com/pod-product-compliance
Lightning Source LLC
Chambersburg PA
CBHW051506120626
46551CB00012B/805